SADLIER
Sacrament Program

# The Spirit Sets Us Free

## Confirmation Preparation for Youth

D1406836

**Project Director**
Linda Gaupin, C.D.P., Ph.D.

**Collaborator**
JoAnn Paradise, D.Min.

**Consultants**
Rev. Msgr. John F. Barry
Rev. Virgil P. Elizondo, Ph.D., S.T.D.
Rev. James A. Field
Rev. James P. Moroney
Rev. J-Glenn Murray, S.J.
Maureen Sullivan, O.P., Ph.D.
Nicholas Wagner

**Publisher**
Gerard F. Baumbach, Ed.D.

**Editor in Chief**
Moya Gullage

**Official Theological Consultant**
Most Rev. Edward K. Braxton, Ph.D., S.T.D.
Auxiliary Bishop of St. Louis

**Product Developer**
Michaela Burke

**Contributors**
Gloria Hutchinson
Helen Hemmer, I.H.M.

William H. Sadlier, Inc.
9 Pine Street
New York, N Y   10005-1002

**Nihil Obstat**
Sister Lucy Vazquez, O.P.
*Censor Librorum*

**Imprimatur**
✠ Most Reverend Norbert M. Dorsey, C.P.
Bishop of Orlando
July 15, 1999

The *Nihil Obstat* and *Imprimatur* are official
declarations that a book or pamphlet is free of
doctrinal or moral error. No implication is contained
therein that those who have granted the *Nihil Obstat*
and *Imprimatur* agree with the contents, opinions or
statements expressed.

Printed in the United States of America.

**𝕊** is a registered trademark of William H. Sadlier, Inc.

Home Office:
9 Pine Street
New York, NY 10005–1002

ISBN: 0-8215-5701-7

12131415/08 07 06

## Acknowledgements

Scripture excerpts are taken from the *New American Bible with Revised New Testament and Psalms* Copyright © 1991, 1986, 1970 Confraternity of Christian Doctrine, Inc., Washington, DC. Used with permission. All rights reserved. No part of the *New American Bible* may be used or reproduced in any form, without permission in writing from the copyright owner.

Excerpts from the English translation of the *Catechism of the Catholic Church* for use in the United States of America, Copyright © 1994, United States Catholic Conference, Inc.— Libreria Editrice Vaticana.

Excerpts from the English translation of *Rite of Baptism for Children* © 1969, International Committee on English in the Liturgy, Inc. (ICEL); excerpts from the English translation of *The Roman Missal* © 1973, ICEL; excerpts from the English translation of *Rite of Confirmation, 2nd edition* © 1975, ICEL; excerpts from the English translation of *A Book of Prayers* © 1982, ICEL; excerpts from the English translation of *Rite of Christian Initiation of Adults* © 1985, ICEL. All rights reserved.

English translation of the Nicene Creed by the International Consultation on English Texts, (ICET). The prayer, "God we pray for our young people . . . " © Church Hymnal Corporation.

Cover Illustrator: Diane Fenster

# CONTENTS

## 1
# BORN ANEW IN BAPTISM

### page 6

*Opening Prayer:* Make us children of light!
*Key Terms:* sacrament, sanctifying grace, Baptism
*Symbol Talk:* water, light; white garment
*The Pope and You-th:* Do you know what Baptism does to you?

## 2
# SEALED WITH THE GIFT OF THE SPIRIT

### page 18

*Opening Prayer:* Excite us with a renewed
understanding of the Spirit!
*Key Terms:* sacraments of initiation, Confirmation
*Symbol Talk:* cloud and light
*The Church and You-th:* actions of confirmed Catholics

---

**page 30**

**Walk with Me:** Choosing a Sponsor

---

## 3
# IN THE STRENGTH OF HIS LOVE

### page 32

*Opening Prayer:* May we spread the faith by word and action.
*Key Terms:* gifts of the Holy Spirit
*Symbol Talk:* laying on of hands
*The Pope and You-th:* Be witnesses to the gospel!

# 4
# THE OIL OF SALVATION

**page 44**

*Opening Prayer:* Transform us into the likeness of Christ.
*Key Terms:* chrism, Christ
*Symbol Talk:* anointing with oil
*The Pope and You-th:* Undertake the Lord's
mission right where you are!

# 5
# MORE LIKE CHRIST

**page 56**

*Opening Prayer:* "I am the vine, you are the branches."
*Key Terms:* incarnation, gospel
*The Pope and You-th:* The gospel is life!
Bear witness to this life.

# 6
# IN THE UNITY OF FAITH

**page 68**

*Opening Prayer:* We are one body in Christ.
*Key Terms:* Eucharist, Communion, liturgy
*Symbol Talk:* the breaking of bread
*The Church and You-th:* a young person's prayer

**page 80**

**Confirmation Retreat**
Theme: The Holy Spirit—Giver of Life

**page 86**

**Called by Name**
Choosing a Confirmation Name

**page 88**

**I Believe**
A Summary of Basic Beliefs

**page 92**          **page 94**          **page 96**
**Prayers**          **Glossary**          **Index**

# Born Anew
# in Baptism

We believe in you, Lord Jesus Christ.
Fill our hearts with your radiance,
and make us children of light!

Song from Ancient Liturgy

## ❧ OPENING PRAYER ❧

**Entrance Song:** *(Use the entrance song that will be sung at Confirmation.)*

**Leader:** In the name of the Father, and of the Son, and of the Holy Spirit.

**R/.** Amen.

**Leader:** Brothers and sisters, give praise to God, who sends us the Holy Spirit to live in our hearts and has favored us in wonderful ways. Blessed be God now and for ever.

**R/.** Amen.

**Leader:** Let us pray that we may be renewed by the grace of our Baptism: *(Silence)*

Almighty and eternal God, in Baptism you gave new life in the Spirit to your sons and daughters.

In spirit and power,
keep all who are reborn of water and the Spirit
your adopted children,
and may we always proclaim with our lips
the good news of salvation.

Renew within us the power of our Baptism
and fill us with zeal for your gospel.
Strengthen us to acknowledge Christ,
so that we who are born in his likeness
may journey on the path of salvation
begun in our Baptism.

We ask this through Christ our Lord.

**R/.** Amen.

### LITURGY OF THE WORD

**Reading:** Ezekiel 36:24–30

**Responsorial Psalm:** *(Use the responsorial psalm that will be sung at Confirmation.)*

**Gospel Acclamation:** *(Use the gospel acclamation that will be sung at Confirmation.)*

**Gospel:** John 3:1–6

**Reflection** (an explanation of God's word in the readings)

## Blessing

Leader: *(Invites the candidates to kneel)*
On the day of your Baptism the Christian
community
welcomed you with great joy.
You were baptized in the name of the Father,
and of the Son, and of the Holy Spirit.
You put on the Lord Jesus.

Today we give you a cross as a reminder that you
were claimed for Christ, and we pray that God's
blessing be upon you.
*Catholic Household Blessings and Prayers*

R/. Amen.

Leader: I invite all those preparing to receive
Confirmation to come forward to accept the
cross.

Catechist[s]: *(Gives each person a cross and says the
following prayer.)*

Blessed be God who chose you in Christ.

R/. Amen.

## General Intercessions

Leader: We ask God to accompany us on our
journey and pray for the needs of all God's
adopted children. Our response will be:
*Lord, hear our prayer.*

**1.** We have been marked by the sign of the cross.
Give us the courage to live this sign in our world.
We pray to the Lord.

**2.** We have rejected Satan. Strengthen us to
proclaim the Good News of salvation in our
world today. We pray to the Lord.

**3.** We have accepted the light of Christ. Help us
to keep this flame of faith alive in our hearts.
We pray to the Lord.

**4.** We have experienced your living waters. Fill
us with the desire to grow in the likeness of Christ.
We pray to the Lord.

**5.** We have worn the white robe of salvation.
May we continue to clothe ourselves in Christ.
We pray to the Lord.

**6.** We have been named children of God. Open
our hearts to accept and love all God's children.
We pray to the Lord.

Leader: God, the giver of all life,
hear the prayers of those who have been reborn
to everlasting life.
Be with us on our journey as we deepen our love
for your Spirit.
We ask this through Christ our Lord.

R/. Amen.

Leader: Gathered as one body in Christ, let us
pray in the words that Jesus gave us:

All: Our Father . . . .

## CONCLUSION

Leader: God of salvation,
you revealed to Nicodemus a new birth
in water and the Spirit
and called him and us to be born
in the likeness of your Son, Jesus Christ.
Awaken our faith in your Word dwelling
among us.
Give us a renewed sense of all Christian life
as a continual, day after day, living out of our
Baptism.
We ask this through Christ our Lord.

R/. Amen.

Leader: *(Signs himself or herself with the sign of
the cross and says:)*
May God the Father, with the Son and the Holy
Spirit, be praised and blessed for ever and ever.

R/. Amen.

*R*enew within us the powers of our Baptism and fill us with zeal for your gospel. Strengthen us to acknowledge Christ, so that we who are born in his likeness may journey in the path of salvation begun in our Baptism.

**Such wonderful words! Among other things we ask for in the prayer is strength to continue our journey on the path of salvation. Do you ever think of your Christian life as a journey towards salvation? In what ways?**

Every time I pray, I am seeking guidance in hope to better understand the path to salvation.

## Born Anew

Baptism is truly the beginning of our journey. Most of us were baptized as infants. It is through the Church that we receive faith and new life in Christ. In Baptism we are born anew and we set out "on the path of salvation." But what does that really mean? Someone once asked Jesus that same question.

The Gospel of John tells of a man called Nicodemus, an important member of the Jewish Sanhedrin, who comes at night to Jesus to whom he says:

"Rabbi, we know that you are a teacher who has come from God, for no one can do these signs that you are doing unless God is with him." Jesus answered and said to him, "Amen, amen, I say to you, no one can see the kingdom of God without being born from above." Nicodemus said to him, "How can a person once grown old be born again? Surely he cannot reenter his mother's womb and be born again, can he?"

Jesus makes Nicodemus move from what he can see to the much deeper reality—things he cannot see with his eyes. Nicodemus at first can only deal with the visible: We are born once of a mother and father. How can we be born again? But Jesus came to show us all a much deeper truth: through him we are to experience a different birth, a spiritual birth. And so he answers Nicodemus' question:

"Amen, amen, I say to you, no one can enter the kingdom of God without being born of water and Spirit. What is born of flesh is flesh and what is born of the Spirit is spirit" (John 3:2–6).

At your Baptism you were born "of water and the Spirit." You died to your "old life"—you died to original sin. *Original sin* is the rejection of God by our first parents, resulting in the loss of sanctifying grace for themselves and all their decendants. Because of original sin, human nature is weakened and inclined to sin. But we have been saved by Jesus Christ and restored to a life of grace. Jesus, true God and true Man, the incarnation of the second Person of the Blessed Trinity, saved us from sin by his life, death, and resurrection.

Baptism is the sacrament of your new birth, your new life in Christ. And the sacramental sign of that new life is the life-giving water of Baptism.

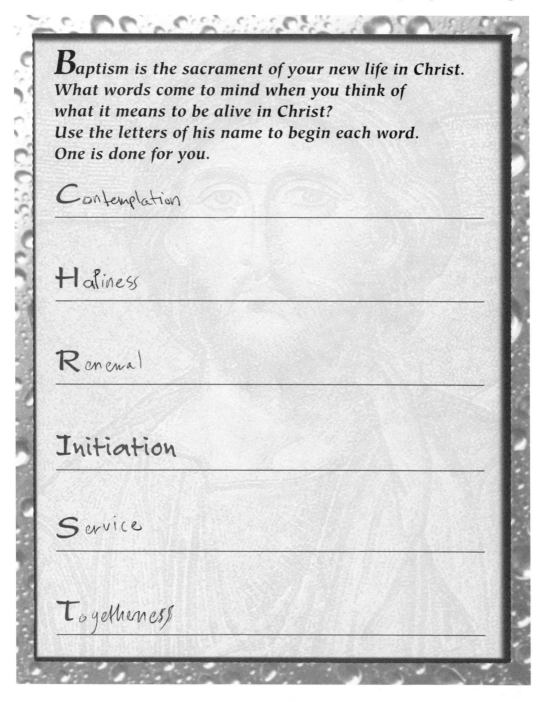

*Baptism is the sacrament of your new life in Christ.*
*What words come to mind when you think of*
*what it means to be alive in Christ?*
*Use the letters of his name to begin each word.*
*One is done for you.*

Contemplation

Holiness

Renewal

Initiation

Service

Togetherness

# The Waters of Life

What images come to mind when you hear the word "water"? Do you think of a cold drink that relieves thirst? Perhaps you see images of a peaceful lake or the powerful surf of the ocean. You might think of spring rains that renew the earth and make even the desert bloom. Water is a source of life for all things, but especially for us. It makes up 60% of our bodies and is crucial to our survival.

Water, so essential for life, is the key symbol of Baptism, the sacrament of our new life in God. At the Easter Vigil, before those preparing for Baptism are initiated into the Church, the water for Baptism is blessed. The celebrant prays that God the Father will give us grace through the sign of the gift of water. We recall together God's saving acts, especially those involving water. And we pray that all who are buried with Christ in Baptism may rise with him to new life.

Those who are to be baptized are then plunged into the water (or water is poured over their heads), and the priest or deacon baptizes them in the name of the Father, and of the Son, and of the Holy Spirit.

This immersion gives the sacrament its name, for *to baptize* comes from a Greek word that means "to plunge into" or "to immerse." In Baptism the water is a symbol of Christ's death and rising. The newly baptized are plunged into his death and come up from the water risen with Christ—and now all is new. Baptismal life is forever.

As a sign of this new life the newly baptized are anointed on the head with chrism, or holy oil, and are clothed with a white garment to signify that they have "become a new creation;" they are now clothed in Christ.

This is what took place at your Baptism, too.

*Imagine that you are about to be baptized. Think of three things that you would like to have "made new" in your life.*

Write them here.

## Children of Light

Another powerful symbol of Baptism is light. At your Baptism a lighted candle was given to you. "Receive the light of Christ," the celebrant said. Then he prayed:

> You have been enlightened by Christ. Walk always as children of the light and keep the flame of faith alive in your hearts.

Unlike the candle that is extinguished at the end of the liturgy, the spiritual light that we receive at Baptism is the very life of God. It burns within us, changing us forever. We are filled with God's own life through the power of the Holy Spirit. This is what is called *sanctifying grace*. This light can only be extinguished by a free choice of ours to reject God.

At Baptism we promise to follow the path of salvation. Our light and our guide on that path is Christ himself.

Pope John Paul II who wants the young people of the world to understand more deeply and commit themselves more completely to the life they share in Christ, said recently:

> "Dear young people, do you know what the sacrament of Baptism does to you? God acknowledges you as his children and transforms your existence into a story of love with him. He conforms you to Christ so that you will be able to fulfill your personal vocation. He has come to make a pact with you, and he offers you his peace. Live from now on as children of the light who know they are reconciled by the cross of the Savior."

drink
clean
bathe
cool
gives new life

warmth
fuel
heat
cooking
light
burn stuff
forever
engine

### Key Terms

The Church challenges us as baptized Christians to be living witnesses to Christ in our world. If we are to do this, if we are to proclaim the faith clearly, we must first understand the words that express it. Here are a few simple terms. Learn them by heart.

**sacrament:** a visible and effective sign, given to us by Christ, through which we share in God's grace

**sanctifying grace:** a participation in the very life of God that brings us into an intimate and permanent relationship with the Blessed Trinity; we first receive this divine gift at Baptism

**Baptism:** the sacrament in which we are freed from original sin, given a share in God's life, and welcomed as members of the Church

*Think for a moment: In Baptism your very existence was transformed into a "story of love" with God. What does that mean to you?*

**Symbol TALK**

A symbol suggests something else. It is usually something visible that expresses a truth about an invisible thing. Among all creatures of earth, we humans are the only ones who have the power and the imagination to think symbolically, to interpret and make sense of our lives, and to express in symbols our deepest beliefs and concerns.

What do these symbols express about the sacrament of Baptism?

**water**   renewal of life
cleansing
connects us
refreshing

**candle**   warmth
life of God
illumination

**white garment**
healing
purity
blank slate

## The Power of Baptism

Today we prayed, "Renew within us the power of our Baptism." What is this power? What does it do in us? Saint Paul tells us:

> "Or are you unaware that we who were baptized into Christ Jesus were baptized into his death? We were indeed buried with him through baptism into death, so that, just as Christ was raised from the dead by the glory of the Father, we too might live in newness of life."
> Romans 6:3–4

It seems strange to say that we must "die" with Christ in order to live. Saint Paul gives us the meaning: going down into the cleansing waters of Baptism is not an empty symbol; it is a powerful, effective sign of our immersion in, our union with Jesus Christ. We, the baptized, are given a share in his resurrection, his new life.

When we pray "Renew in us the power of our Baptism," we are asking for the strength, the courage, the desire to be true disciples of Jesus.

Through all these baptismal symbols the Church expresses its belief that "Baptism is the basis of the whole Christian life, the gateway to life in the Spirit . . . and the door which gives access to the other sacraments" (*Catechism of the Catholic Church*, 1213). It is the beginning of our initiation into the Church—an initiation that is sealed and nourished by two other sacraments: Confirmation and Eucharist. For this reason these three sacraments are called the *sacraments of initiation*. In a very real way a Baptism, Confirmation, and Eucharist can be thought of as "one moment."

In celebrating this "moment," we signify our willingness to turn from selfishness and sin to a life in the Spirit of Christ Jesus. We are in Christ and Christ is in us. His work, his mission, is now our own.

*Have you discovered in this session something about Baptism that you did not know before? Share it.*

## The Pope & YOUth

When thousands of Catholic youth journeyed to Paris, France in August 1997, Pope John Paul II asked them "Do you know what Baptism does to you?"

The Holy Father then reminded them that Baptism
• brings us into intimacy with God.
• purifies us from sin and opens us to a new future.
• is a bath which washes and regenerates.
• is a vestment of strength and perfection.

Then the pope assured the young people:

> "Baptism is the sign that God has joined us on our journey, that he makes our existence more beautiful and that he transforms our history into a history of holiness."

# MAPPING

## POINTS OF DEPARTURE

Why do we speak of Baptism as the beginning of our journey on the path of salvation?

SYMBOLS ON THE MAP

What truths about Baptism does the symbol of water help us to understand?

## Destination Points

**Let's discuss:**

As a young Catholic preparing for Confirmation, what will you do to live out your baptismal identity this week?

Name one specific way you will show, in the family, the parish, or the community, that you have been born in the likeness of Christ.

# THE JOURNEY

**Reflections**

Through Baptism the Holy Spirit dwells in me and remains with me always.

*My Prayer:*

Holy Spirit, help me to remember that I am never without your care and protection. I pray today that *My parents don't feel lonely*

## closing *Prayer*

Father of love and power
it is your will to establish everything in Christ
and to draw us into his all-embracing love.

Guide these chosen ones:
strengthen them in their vocation,
build them into the kingdom of your Son,
and seal them with the Spirit of your promise.

We ask this through Christ our Lord.
Amen.

*The Rite of Baptism*

# Sealed with the Gift of the Spirit

Lord, send out your Spirit, and renew the face of the earth.

The Rite of Confirmation

# ~ OPENING PRAYER ~

**Entrance Song:** *(Use the entrance song that will be sung at Confirmation.)*

**Leader:** In the name of the Father, and of the Son, and of the Holy Spirit.

**R/.** Amen.

**Leader:** *(greets those present in the following words)*

Brothers and sisters, give praise to God, who sends us the Holy Spirit to live in our hearts and has favored us in wonderful ways. Blessed be God now and for ever.

**R/.** Amen.

**Leader:** Let us pray for the Gift of the Spirit in our lives: *(Silence)*

God of power and mercy,
you sent your Spirit upon the disciples
and set their hearts on fire with love.
Send your Spirit to live in our hearts,
and excite in us a renewed
understanding of the Spirit in our lives.

We ask this through Christ our Lord.

**R/.** Amen.

## LITURGY OF THE WORD

**Reading:** Acts 2:1–6, 22b–23, 32–33

**Responsorial Psalm:** *(Use the responsorial psalm that will be sung at Confirmation.)*

**Gospel Acclamation:** *(Use the gospel acclamation that will be sung at Confirmation.)*

**Gospel:** John 7:37–39

**Reflection**

**Blessing**

**Leader:** *(Invites the candidates to kneel and prays:)*

On the day of your Baptism
your parents were entrusted to keep the light
   of Christ burning brightly in your lives.
When you were baptized in the name of
   the Father,
and of the Son, and of the Holy Spirit
you were enlightened by Christ.

Today we pass this flame of faith to you
   once again,
so that you will always remember
that you are to walk as children of the light
   in this world,
and we pray that God's blessing be upon you.

**R/.** Amen.

**Leader:** I invite all those preparing to receive Confirmation to come forward to receive the flame of faith.

**Catechist(s)** *(Standing beside the paschal candle, gives each candidate a candle, lit with the flame from the paschal candle, and says:)*

Receive this light and keep it alive in your hearts.

R/. Amen.

## General Intercessions

**Leader:** We ask God to accompany us on our journey and pray that the Spirit will help us to be his witnesses before the world. Our response is *Lord, hear our prayer.*

**1.** We know your Spirit in the symbol of living waters. Give us *wisdom* so that we may continue to live our call to holiness in this world.
We pray to the Lord.

**2.** We know your Spirit in the anointing with oil. Give us *courage* to remain forever faithful to Christ who is priest, prophet, and king.
We pray to the Lord.

**3.** We know your Spirit in the symbol of *fire*. Give us *knowledge* to keep the flame of faith alive in our hearts.
We pray to the Lord.

**4.** We know your Spirit in the symbols of *cloud* and *light*. Give us *understanding* to accept your revelation as the living and saving God.
We pray to the Lord.

**5.** We know your Spirit in the *laying on of hands*. Give us *right judgment* so that we may discern the outpouring of your Spirit in our lives.
We pray to the Lord.

**6.** We know your Spirit as *breath, air,* and *wind*—the breath of God, the divine Spirit.
We are filled with *wonder* and *awe* and ask that you place this gift within our hearts.
We pray to the Lord.

**7.** We know your Spirit in the symbol of the *dove*. Give us *reverence* so that we may respect the signs and symbols of your presence in this world.
We pray to the Lord.

**8.** (Add your group petition.)

**Leader:** God, the giver of all life,
   you sent your Spirit upon the disciples and set
      their hearts on fire with love.
   Hear the prayers of those who long for your
      Spirit of truth.
   We ask this through Christ our Lord.

R/. Amen.

## Lord's Prayer

**Leader:** Gathered as one body in Christ, let us pray in the words that Jesus gave us:

**All:** Our Father . . . .

## CONCLUSION

**Leader:** Father of light,
   send your Spirit into our lives.
   With the power of a mighty wind
   and by the flame of your wisdom,
   open our minds to your presence.
   Loosen our tongues to sing your praise
   in words beyond the power of speech,
   for without your Spirit we could
   never raise our voices in words of peace
   or announce the truth that Jesus is Lord.

We ask this through Christ our Lord.

R/. Amen.

**Leader:** *(Concludes the rite by signing himself or herself with the sign of the cross and saying:)*

May God the Father, with the Son and the Holy Spirit, be praised and blessed for ever and ever.

R/. Amen.

*E*xcite in us a renewed understanding of the Spirit in our lives.

**As you begin this time of preparation for Confirmation, what is your understanding of the Holy Spirit in your life? Write three words or phrases that come to mind when you think of the Holy Spirit.**

## A Renewed Understanding

Suppose someone asks you the meaning of Confirmation, and says, "Isn't Baptism enough? Why bother with Confirmation?" What would you say? Why are you here in this group preparing for Confirmation? Do you think it is important? Do you think it will change you in any way?

Perhaps a little history will help us understand more clearly the meaning of Confirmation. From the early days of the Church the sacraments of initiation—Baptism, Confirmation, and Eucharist—were celebrated in one event at the Easter Vigil. Coming out of the baptismal waters the newly baptized were sealed with the Gift of the Holy Spirit by the laying on of hands. This Gift of the Spirit completed the grace of Baptism. In addition, to signify this Gift, a person was anointed with holy oil. This laying on of hands and anointing were the origin of the sacrament of Confirmation in the Catholic Church.

To complete this initiation, after Baptism and Confirmation, the new Christians were invited to the table of the Lord to celebrate Eucharist for the first time. Today the Church uses the same sequence of sacraments in receiving adults into the Church. So why are you celebrating Confirmation at your age?

As the Church grew something happened to Confirmation. Infant Baptism became more common, and was celebrated throughout the year. Gradually, the celebration of Confirmation became separated from Baptism and was postponed until a later time.

For you these three sacraments of initiation into the Church have been spread over your lifetime: you were probably baptized as an infant, received the Eucharist at seven or eight, and are now preparing for Confirmation. Sometimes, because of the years separating these sacraments, it is difficult to remember the important relationship among these three sacraments: Baptism cleanses us from original sin and makes us children of God; Confirmation seals us with the Spirit, strengthening the grace of Baptism; Eucharist nourishes and sustains our new life in Christ.

Baptism makes us members of Christ's body, a change so radical that it can never be undone. It seals us with a spiritual mark, or character, that cannot be taken away. In Confirmation the Holy Spirit incorporates us more firmly into Christ, increasing the grace of Baptism and strengthening our bond with the Church. Confirmation, too, marks us with an indelible character that cannot be repeated. We are signed with Christ, sealed with the Gift of the Spirit forever. Because Baptism, Confirmation, and Eucharist form a unity as the sacraments of initiation, Confirmation is for you the final sacrament of your Christian initiation.

*In ancient times, a seal was a symbol of a significant person, a sign of that person's authority or ownership. Soldiers were marked with the seal of their leader, for example, to show that their total loyalty was to him; they would follow him forever. Soon you will receive the seal of the Holy Spirit in Confirmation. If you could visualize the "seal of the Spirit," what images or words would appear to show that you belong to Christ?*

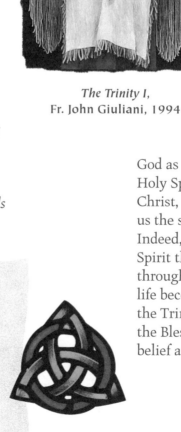

*The Trinity I,*
Fr. John Giuliani, 1994

## Signs of the Spirit

Let's take a closer look at who the Holy Spirit really is. To do that we need to examine the word *spirit* itself. It's a difficult word to define. If you say, for example, that your school or your team has "spirit," what do you mean? If a person is said to bring "spirit" to another, or if we describe someone as "spiritual," what are we actually saying? Perhaps words like enthusiasm, energy, commitment, or comfort come to mind.

These words, and others, can also help us to understand the Holy Spirit. It is important to remember, however, that the Holy Spirit is more than just a word, more than just an experience, more than just a symbol. The Holy Spirit is a Person, the Third Person of the Blessed Trinity.

How astonishing! This means that in Confirmation we are not just learning more about God, not just going through a rite—we are entering into a much closer relationship with the Trinity.

As Saint Paul points out, the Holy Spirit allows us to cry out "Abba" to God the Father, acknowledging God as Father as Jesus did (Romans 8:15). The Holy Spirit brings us into a stronger union with Christ, the fullness of God's revelation, and gives us the strength to proclaim his name boldly. Indeed, it is through the power of the Holy Spirit that we are able to worship the Father through the Son. In a wonderful way, then, our life becomes intimately bound up with the life of the Trinity. It is thus easy to understand why the Blessed Trinity lies at the center of Christian belief and of the Christian life.

23

If we truly understand this, then the words of Scripture come alive for us and the promise of Jesus to send us a Helper becomes real. Look at the words of Jesus and the words that have come down to us from the experience of the early Church.
The Spirit is:

- *Advocate* (John 14:16)
One who speaks on our behalf, defends us, comforts and consoles us

- *Spirit of truth* (John 14:17)
One who communicates God's truth, inspires the Scriptures, guides our faith journey

- *Spirit of glory* (1 Peter 4:14)
One who urges us on to the glory God has in store for us and who gives us the courage to share in Jesus' mission.

This is the Holy Spirit who is poured forth in us in Confirmation.

**Symbol TALK**

As we have seen breath, wind, and fire tell us of the Spirit. In the Scriptures and the liturgy, we find other symbols that make the Spirit's presence known.

*Cloud and light* are signs of God's saving presence and glory. In the Old Testament, the Hebrews, fleeing slavery in Egypt, were led by God through the desert with a column of cloud by day and a column of fire by night. When Moses went to speak to God in the meeting tent, a cloud would appear before the entrance to the tent. Then all the people would go and worship in their own tents knowing that God was present among them (Exodus 33:9–10).

In the New Testament we read that when Jesus was transfigured on the mountain, the Spirit came in a cloud that overshadowed him. The cloud was bright and shone like light on Jesus (Matthew 17:1–8).

On the day of Jesus' ascension a cloud took Jesus out of the sight of the disciples. An angel appeared and told them Jesus would return at the end of the world in the same way (Acts 1:9–11).

Cloud and light are recurring symbols in the Bible of the saving presence of the Holy Spirit.

# In Wind and Fire

The language the Church uses to describe the Holy Spirit is the language of God's revelation to us, the language of Scripture and tradition. *Spirit* is a most interesting word. It is the proper name given to us by God for the Third Person of the Blessed Trinity. The word *spirit* is a translation of the Hebrew word for "breath," "air," or "wind." The Holy Spirit comes to us as the Giver of Life, the very breath of God's life, which is as essential to our spiritual existence as air is essential to our physical life.

On the evening of the first Easter, the disciples were gathered together in a locked room. They were stunned by the events of Jesus' suffering and death and confused by wild rumors and messages that he had risen and appeared to Mary Magdalen and some women. Then the risen Jesus stood among them. He breathed on them and said, "Receive the holy Spirit" (John 20:22). The breath of Christ who had overcome fear and suffering and death itself stirred the souls of the apostles to new life.

*Can you think of a time or an experience in which you felt the presence of God's Spirit breathing new life into you?*

One rich symbol for the Holy Spirit is fire. Fire suggests warmth, light, energy, power. Fire changes forever what it touches; it consumes and it energizes. Jesus said, "I have come to set the earth on fire, and how I wish it were already blazing!" (Luke 12:49).

That was his mission: to transform the world, to set it on fire with God's love. And so he sent the Holy Spirit upon his disciples in flames of fire, filling them with zeal and energy and courage to continue his work.

*Pentecost,* Andrea di Cione Orcagna, 14th century

25

## The Spirit in Us

So why are we confirmed? And what does it mean to have the Holy Spirit in our lives? To get a clue think again of the idea that we are "sealed with the Gift of the Spirit." The Spirit seals us; the Spirit changes us; the Spirit transforms us. We become more of what Christ calls us to be—like himself. The Holy Spirit enables us not only to understand Christ's life, but to make Christ's life our own.

Think of the activity of the Holy Spirit in the life of the Church and in your own life. Think, for example, of Mass. We hear the priest say in the Liturgy of the Eucharist, "Let your Spirit come upon these gifts" and we realize that the bread and wine will be transformed. They will become the Body and Blood of Christ. We do not see this with our eyes but know it in faith.

At the first Pentecost the disciples had been praying and waiting for the Spirit whom Jesus had promised. They lacked the courage and the wisdom they needed to fulfill Jesus' mission—to make disciples of all nations. Suddenly, without warning, the house in which they had gathered was filled with the rush of a strong wind, a wind that would sweep their doubts and fears away. Then flaming tongues of fire appeared above each one. "And they were all filled with the holy Spirit and began to speak in different tongues, as the Spirit enabled them to proclaim" (Acts 2:4).

As he had promised, Jesus poured forth upon them the Holy Spirit, whom he had received from the Father. And the Spirit transformed the disciples into fiery evangelizers who, on that amazing first day alone, baptized three thousand new Christians. Today the Holy Spirit still enlivens the Church: the Church is brought alive in the Holy Spirit, who is poured out on all the members of the Church. It is the Holy Spirit who builds the Church and keeps it vital and dynamic.

And now that same Spirit will come upon you in Confirmation bringing you the same gifts the disciples received and enabling you, as it enabled them, to be witnesses to Christ.

There is a transformation about to take place in your life. When you are confirmed, you will be changed, transformed, by the power of the Holy Spirit. How will you recognize this transformation? Through the grace of Confirmation you will find that you can have the courage to withstand negative peer pressure, and to share your faith without fear or embarrassment.

How amazing! In Confirmation the Holy Spirit will come upon you to strengthen God's life in you, and to fill you with enthusiasm and energy for Christ's mission. The Holy Spirit does not force you, however. You must do your part—you must be open to the presence of the Spirit; you must cooperate with the gifts the Spirit brings you and the work the Spirit wishes to accomplish in you. Confirmation does not produce immediate maturity and holiness. What it *does* do is give us the power, the energy to grow and mature day-by-day, year-by-year so as to finally reach our full potential in Christ.

# The Church & YOUth

In a "Message to Youth," the bishops of the United States expressed their esteem and respect for young people in whom they "see the face of God." Calling on young people to recognize their own value, the bishops said, "You are made in the image and likeness of God. You are loved by God and others!"

Out of this great love, in which you will soon be confirmed by the Holy Spirit, comes action. Here are seven actions the Church asks young people to undertake as witness to Christ:

✓ work for justice and peace;
✓ treat others with respect;
✓ share your time and talents;
✓ be a healer when conflicts arise;
✓ help friends do the right thing;
✓ befriend youth who are lonely;
✓ value those who are different.

The bishops added, "We're not saying it will be easy. You may be misunderstood and ridiculed at times but you will never be alone. Christ and the Christian community walk with you."

*Which of these actions are you already trying to carry out in your life? Have you encountered any criticism or ridicule for your actions?*

# MAPPING

## POINTS OF DEPARTURE

How would you explain the meaning of the Holy Spirit in our lives? What changes does the Spirit have the power to make in our lives through Confirmation?

Define:

**sacraments of initiation:** *reception and sealing of gift of Holy Spirit*

**Confirmation:** *gift of holy spirit is sealed*

## SYMBOLS ON THE MAP

What truths about the Spirit and Confirmation do the symbols of wind and fire communicate?

How does the symbol of cloud and light increase your understanding of the Spirit in your life?

## Destination Points

**Let's discuss:**

As a young Catholic on the road to Confirmation, what will you do to prepare to "be sealed with the Gift of the Holy Spirit"?

Choose one of the seven actions suggested by the U.S. bishops in their "Message to Youth" that you most need to work on. Tell why.

## JOURNAL NOTES

### Reflections

The anointing with oil and the words *Be sealed with the Gift of the Holy Spirit* mark me forever as a witness to the gospel.

### My Prayer:

Holy Spirit, I know I am called to witness to Christ wherever I am. This isn't easy. I need your help to

### closing *Prayer*

Father of light,
send your Spirit into our lives.
With the power of a mighty wind
and by the flame of your wisdom
open the horizons of our minds.
Loosen our tongues to sing your praise,
for without your Spirit
we could never raise our voices
    in words of peace
or announce the truth that Jesus is Lord.
Amen.

# Walk with Me:
## Choosing a Sponsor

### Why a Sponsor?

From the earliest days of the Church, those seeking communion with the Church were supported by specific people chosen from the community. At your Baptism those significant people were your parents and godparents (your baptismal sponsors) who promised that you would be raised in the faith. They professed *their* faith because you could not speak for yourself. Your parents accepted the responsibility of training you in the practice of the faith. Your godparents promised to help your parents. In Confirmation you will speak for yourself; you will renew your baptismal promises. You will be supported by a sponsor who will stand with you and present you to the bishop for Confirmation.

### Choosing a Sponsor

The Church encourages you to choose, if possible, one of your baptismal godparents to be your sponsor for Confirmation because this expresses more clearly the link between your Baptism and Confirmation. This person would be a good choice if she/he:

✦ has been close enough to you to have been supportive of your life so far;

✦ is a baptized Catholic who has received Eucharist and has been confirmed;

✦ is a practicing Catholic who participates in the Eucharistic celebration every Sunday;

✦ lives a good Catholic life;

✦ is at least 16 years of age.

## Role of a Sponsor

The person you ask to be your sponsor should know you well enough to be able to testify, by his or her presence before the community, that you are someone who wishes to be fully incorporated into the Church as a believing, practicing Catholic; that you are one who takes part faithfully in the Church's worship, witness, and mission. When you are anointed with the chrism during Confirmation your sponsor will be beside you with a hand placed on your shoulder. This is sign of your spiritual relationship.

If you have not yet chosen your sponsor, now is an excellent time to think about your choice. Ask yourself:

○ Is this person someone with whom I feel comfortable?

○ Does this person live near enough to me to truly be able to be a guide and a support?

○ Will this person be willing and able to be my sponsor–to take an active role in my faith life?

Think of one or two people you might choose. Write their names. Then jot down some thoughts about each in the writing box. Use your reflections as a way to make your decision.

**Names:**

**Notes:**

Then write or call the person you have chosen. Talk about your preparation for Confirmation and ask if he or she would be your sponsor. When the person accepts, provide the information about your preparation sessions and, if possible, send him or her, a copy of your text *The Spirit Sets Us Free.* Be sure your sponsor can attend any special sessions for the rite of Confirmation your parish provides and send an invitation including the date, place, and time for the celebration of the sacrament.

## My Confirmation Sponsor is

In the Strength of
His Love

Spirit of truth promised by Christ,
open our minds and hearts
so that we may spread the faith
by word and action.

# OPENING PRAYER

**Entrance Song:** *(Use the entrance song that will be sung at Confirmation.)*

**Leader:** In the name of the Father, and of the Son, and of the Holy Spirit.

**R/. Amen.**

**Leader:** Brothers and sisters, give praise to God who sends us the Holy Spirit
to live in our hearts and has favored us
in wonderful ways.
Blessed be God now and for ever.

**R/. Amen.**

**Leader:** Let us pray. *(Silence)*

Lord,
send us your Holy Spirit
that we may grow in the strength of your love
to the full stature of Christ.
We ask this through Christ our Lord.

**R/. Amen.**

## LITURGY OF THE WORD

**Reading:** Acts 8:4–7, 14–17

**Responsorial Psalm:** *(Use the responsorial psalm that will be sung at Confirmation.)*

**Gospel Acclamation:** *(Use the acclamation that will be sung at Confirmation.)*

**Gospel:** Mark 10:13–16

**Reflection**

## BLESSING

*(The catechist(s) for the candidates come forward.)*

**Leader:** On the day of your Baptism
the Christian community welcomed
you with great joy
and promised to nourish and support
you in the faith.
As you receive this blessing,
know that our community supports you
in this journey of faith,
and prays that you will grow in the
strength of his love.

**R/. Amen.**

*(Those preparing for Confirmation come forward. Extending a sign of peace to each candidate, the catechist(s) prays the following prayer.)*

(N.) In Baptism you were claimed for Christ. May God bless you now and watch over you.

R/. Amen.

## General Intercessions

Leader: Let us be one in prayer to God our Father as we are one in the faith, hope, and love his Spirit gives. Our response is *Lord, hear our prayer.*

1. For these sons and daughters of God, that they may grow in the strength of God's love, we pray to the Lord.

2. For the *wisdom* to see God's plan in our lives, we pray to the Lord.

3. For *understanding,* that we may learn to love all people, we pray to the Lord.

4. For *right judgment* in the choices we make in our lives, we pray to the Lord.

5. For the *courage* to live out the gospel message in the world, we pray to the Lord.

6. For the *knowledge* to see God in everything we do, we pray to the Lord.

7. For *reverence,* that we may treat everything that God has made with love and respect, we pray to the Lord.

8. For *wonder and awe* in God's presence, that we may marvel at the work of God's hands in this world, we pray to the Lord.

9. (Add your group petition.)

Leader: God our Father,
you sent your Holy Spirit to give us the gifts
of wisdom and understanding,
right judgment and courage,
knowledge and reverence,
wonder and awe.
May we grow to appreciate the meaning of these gifts
in our lives each day.
We ask this through Christ our Lord.

R/. Amen.

## Lord's Prayer

Leader: Gathered as one body in Christ, let us pray in the words that Jesus gave us:

All: Our Father . . . .

## CONCLUSION

Leader: Let us pray: *(Silence)*

O gracious God,
we pray for the treasures of divine life.
Open our minds and hearts
to receive these gifts
so that we may spread the faith by word
    and action,
as true witnesses of Christ,
confess the name of Christ boldly
    throughout the world,
and never be ashamed of his cross.

We ask this through Christ our Lord.

R/. Amen.

Leader: *(Concludes by signing himself or herself with the sign of the cross and saying:)*
May God the Father, with the Son and the Holy Spirit, be praised and blessed for ever and ever.

R/. Amen.

**O**pen our minds and hearts . . .
so that we may spread the faith
by word and action,
as true witnesses of Christ,
confess the name of Christ boldly
throughout the world,
and never be ashamed of his cross.

**Read again the words of our prayer. The prayer speaks of the things the Holy Spirit comes to do in our lives. Circle any words or phrases that stand out for you. What do you think it means to "spread the faith by word and action"? to "confess the name of Jesus boldly"?**

## Witnesses of Christ

You have probably discovered by now that being Jesus' disciple is not an easy thing. When Jesus called his first followers he was very clear about what discipleship would demand of them. He also made it clear that those who followed him, no matter how great the cost, would have fullness of life. He told them, "If anyone wishes to come after me, he must deny himself and take up his cross daily and follow me. For whoever wishes to save his life will lose it, but whoever loses his life for my sake will save it" (Luke 9:23–24).

You may be thinking right now: Take up my cross daily? Lose my life? What does Jesus mean? It's impossible! How can an ordinary person like me do this on my own?

*Isaac Blessing Jacob,* Jusepe de Ribera, (1588–1656)

The wonderful fact is that we are not on our own. We belong to the Church, a worldwide community of believers and disciples. It is the Holy Spirit who strengthens us and supports us, who fills us with life and energy and courage. With the authority of Christ and through the power of the Holy Spirit, the Church makes its members holy through the celebration of the liturgy and the sacraments. It is the Spirit who makes it possible for us to be witnesses to Christ and not be afraid, to live our faith openly and not be "ashamed of his cross."

 *What do you think might cause someone to be ashamed of the cross? Have you ever been in a situation in which you found it difficult to stand up for your belief in Christ?*

## The Gifts the Spirit Gives

From the moment of Pentecost right up to our own day, the community of Jesus Christ has lived the gospel and given witness to it, as Jesus asked. At times of persecution some disciples gave this witness with their very lives. But through every age and in each struggle, the Holy Spirit guided and renewed the Church, leading its members to be true disciples of Jesus.

The Holy Spirit is with us still and in Confirmation the Spirit will come to you with gifts to strengthen you to be true disciples of Jesus Christ.

The reality of the Holy Spirit's special presence in our lives is brought about by powerful words and gestures in the sacrament of Confirmation. One of these gestures goes back in time thousands and thousands of years. It is called the *laying of hands.* This symbolic act has its roots in the Old Testament. It is an ancient sign of blessing—a unique blessing that conveys authority and grace in God's name. In Genesis, for example, the dying Isaac lays his hands on his son's head, passing on to Jacob authority and responsibility for the whole people. This kind of blessing was such a powerful sign that it could not be cancelled or revoked except by God.

The laying of hands was a common practice in the early Church as well. The apostles laid their hands on the first Christians, passing on to them the Gift of the Spirit that they themselves had received at Pentecost.

In the rite of Confirmation the bishop (or a priest who represents the bishop) extends his hands over you and asks the Holy Spirit to come to you with seven special graces or gifts.

The bishop prays . . .

Send your Holy Spirit upon them
to be their Helper and Guide.
Give them the spirit of wisdom and
    understanding,
the spirit of right judgment and courage,
the spirit of knowledge and reverence.
Fill them with the spirit of wonder and
awe in your presence.

The Spirit does not give these gifts as full-blown powers that work in us whether we cooperate or not. If that were true, every confirmed person would be a saint! Rather, they are given to us as graces to be used and nurtured and developed. They are given to us as powers in potential. That means they have to be activated by us. When we begin to use these powers in love, for the service of others, they grow stronger day by day.

The intercessions in today's opening prayer give some suggestions of ways we can do this.

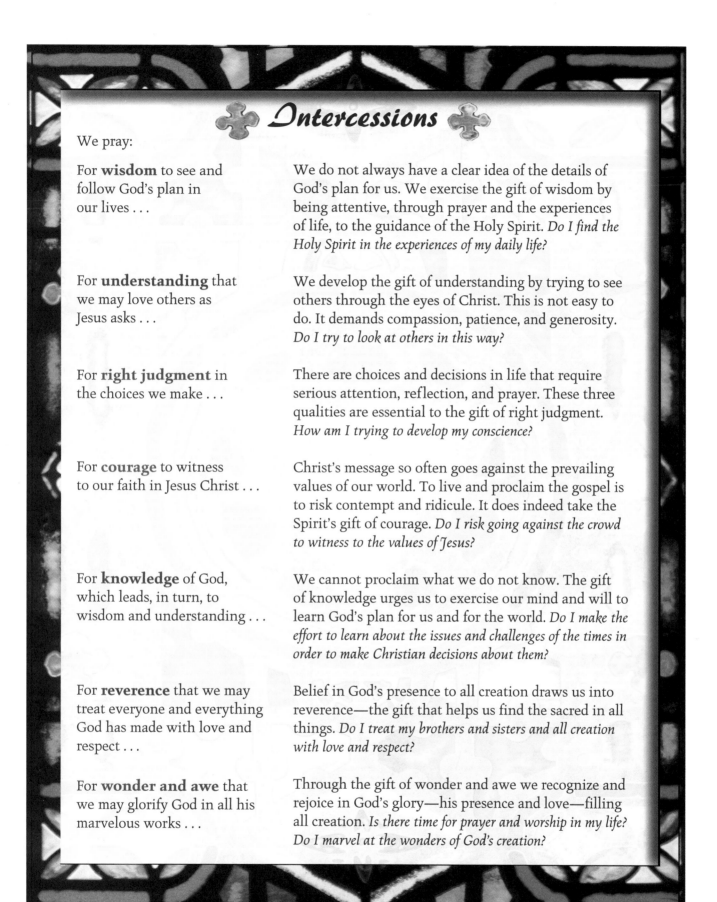

## Intercessions

We pray:

For **wisdom** to see and follow God's plan in our lives . . .

We do not always have a clear idea of the details of God's plan for us. We exercise the gift of wisdom by being attentive, through prayer and the experiences of life, to the guidance of the Holy Spirit. *Do I find the Holy Spirit in the experiences of my daily life?*

For **understanding** that we may love others as Jesus asks . . .

We develop the gift of understanding by trying to see others through the eyes of Christ. This is not easy to do. It demands compassion, patience, and generosity. *Do I try to look at others in this way?*

For **right judgment** in the choices we make . . .

There are choices and decisions in life that require serious attention, reflection, and prayer. These three qualities are essential to the gift of right judgment. *How am I trying to develop my conscience?*

For **courage** to witness to our faith in Jesus Christ . . .

Christ's message so often goes against the prevailing values of our world. To live and proclaim the gospel is to risk contempt and ridicule. It does indeed take the Spirit's gift of courage. *Do I risk going against the crowd to witness to the values of Jesus?*

For **knowledge** of God, which leads, in turn, to wisdom and understanding . . .

We cannot proclaim what we do not know. The gift of knowledge urges us to exercise our mind and will to learn God's plan for us and for the world. *Do I make the effort to learn about the issues and challenges of the times in order to make Christian decisions about them?*

For **reverence** that we may treat everyone and everything God has made with love and respect . . .

Belief in God's presence to all creation draws us into reverence—the gift that helps us find the sacred in all things. *Do I treat my brothers and sisters and all creation with love and respect?*

For **wonder and awe** that we may glorify God in all his marvelous works . . .

Through the gift of wonder and awe we recognize and rejoice in God's glory—his presence and love—filling all creation. *Is there time for prayer and worship in my life? Do I marvel at the wonders of God's creation?*

These gifts of the Holy Spirit are graces that give us the strength to live the moral life. Because of these graces, we are open to follow the promptings of the Holy Spirit. How blessed we are that the Holy Spirit so richly provides us with the strength needed to be followers of Christ.

*Read again Acts 8:14–17 that you heard in today's prayer. Why did Peter and John go to the newly baptized in Samaria?*

## United in Christ

As candidates for the sacrament of Confirmation you are being called to new and more challenging responsibilities. As confirmed members of the Church you must be aware of these obligations. These include:

- participating at Mass on Sundays and holydays
- sharing the faith with others
- learning more about the Church and all its members
- striving for holiness
- living a moral life.

What does it mean to live a moral life? We live a moral life and strive for holiness by freely choosing to live the life of grace given us by God. We have to form our *conscience,* the most basic awareness in us of what is right or wrong. Everyone must follow his or her conscience and form it according to God's law and the teachings of the Church.

Remember that you are not alone; you belong to Christ's body, the Church. The Church teaches with authority because Jesus promised the apostles that the Holy Spirit would call to their minds all that Jesus had taught them. The Holy Spirit continues to guide the successors of the apostles today, the pope and the bishops in communion with him. Christ has given them the power to act in his name.

Jesus does ask difficult things of his followers, but he also promises joy and fullness of life for those who are not ashamed of his cross. The sign of the Christian is the sign of the cross. Saint Paul spoke of the cross to the early Christians. He told them that rather than being ashamed of the cross, we are to "proclaim Christ crucified." Paul went on

### Key Words

**gifts of the spirit:** wisdom, understanding, right judgment, courage, knowledge, reverence, wonder and awe

to say that the cross, when judged by the values of the world is a "stumbling block" but to the eyes of the believer it is the path to holiness and joy (1 Corinthians 1:23).

The reality is that the cross will be present throughout our lives. We will need the Holy Spirit to keep our faith strong when belief is not popular. We will need the Spirit's strength to live the values of Christ when the world says such values are foolish. How do we respond, for example, when the world says it is foolish to care for the needs of the poor, the elderly, the unborn, the terminally ill? It is at times like these when we will truly know what it takes not to be ashamed of his cross.

*Here is something to do privately. Write down one cross that you feel you are being asked to carry right now. Name it as clearly as you can. Then ask the Holy Spirit to help you understand what you must do and to give you the strength to do it.*

## The Pope & YOUth

How can we be disciples of Jesus and witnesses to him in the world? The Holy Father urges you:

Dear young people, your journey does not end here. Time does not come to a halt. Go forth now along the roads of the world, along the pathways of humanity, while remaining ever united in Christ's Church!

Continue to contemplate God's glory and God's love, and you will receive the enlightenment needed to build the civilization of love, to help our brothers and sisters to see the world transfigured by God's eternal wisdom and love.

Be faithful to the Baptism you have received! Be witnesses to the gospel!

*How have you accepted Jesus' challenge to be his disciple? How will it affect your life right now?*

"Journey of Hope," youth rally at the Skydome in Toronto, May, 1993

# MAPPING

## POINTS OF DEPARTURE

What changes can Confirmation bring about in my life?

SYMBOLS ON THE MAP

What does the laying on of hands signify in Confirmation?

## Destination Points

Let's discuss:

Which gifts of the Holy Spirit seem to have the most value to you now? How do you try to use them for yourself and others?

# THE JOURNEY

## JOURNAL NOTES

### Reflections

The Holy Spirit comes to me in Confirmation with seven special graces and gifts that are the sources of strength and courage in my life.

### My Prayer:

Holy Spirit, it's clear to me that I am to use these gifts. I ask you to fill me with zeal and courage so that

## closing Prayer

Lord,
send us your Holy Spirit
to help us walk in unity of faith
and grow in the strength of his love
to the full stature of Christ,
who lives and reigns with you
and the Holy Spirit,
one God, for ever and ever.
Amen.

*The Rite of Confirmation*

# The Oil of Salvation

Loving Father,
you give us the oil of salvation
to transform us into the likeness
of Christ your Son.

The Rite of Confirmation

# OPENING PRAYER

## INTRODUCTION

*Entrance Song:* (*Use the entrance song that will be sung at Confirmation.*)

*Leader:* In the name of the Father, and of the Son, and of the Holy Spirit.

R/. Amen.

*Leader:* (*greets those present in the following words*) Brothers and sisters, give praise to God who sends us the Holy Spirit to live in our hearts and has favored us in wonderful ways. Blessed be God now and for ever.

R/. Amen.

*Leader:* Let us pray. (*Silence*)

God of salvation,
you sent your anointed One into the world
to bring glad tidings to the poor,
liberty to captives,
sight to the blind,
and freedom for the oppressed.
Help us to continue the work
of your anointed One,
and be faithful witnesses to him in this world.
We ask this through Christ our Lord.

R/. Amen.

## LITURGY OF THE WORD

*Reading:* Isaiah 61:1–3a, 6a, 8b–9

*Responsorial Psalm:* (*Use the responsorial psalm that will be sung at Confirmation.*)

*Gospel Acclamation:* (*Use the acclamation that will be sung at Confirmation.*)

*Gospel:* Luke 4:16–22a

*Reflection*

## CHRISM PROCESSION

(*The chrism may be brought forward in solemn procession while an appropriate song is sung. It should be placed on a suitably prepared table in the sanctuary.*)

*Leader:* We bring forth the holy chrism,
which was consecrated by our bishop
during the Chrism Mass
and presented to this local parish
community
with the oil of catechumens and the
oil of the sick.
All who are anointed with the Holy
Spirit
and have been born again in Baptism
are given strength and are transformed
into the likeness of Christ.

## General Intercessions

**Leader:** Christ was anointed priest, prophet, and king. We, too, are anointed in his name and share in his mission. As members of his body let us pray for the needs of all God's people. Our response will be: *Lord, hear our prayer.*

**1.** For those preparing for Baptism: May their anointing with the oil of catechumens deepen their understanding of the gospel and encourage them to accept the challenge of Christian living. We pray to the Lord.

**2.** For those who are seriously ill and have been anointed with the oil of the sick, that they may be healed in body, soul, and spirit. We pray to the Lord.

**3.** For those who were anointed with the oil of chrism at Baptism, that they may remain as temples of your glory and live radiant with joy. We pray to the Lord.

**4.** For those who have been anointed into the priestly service of the Church, that they may remain faithful witnesses in the world. We pray to the Lord.

**5.** For those preparing for Confirmation, that they may be filled with the rich fragrance of Christ. We pray to the Lord.

**6.** For all those who gather to worship within the walls anointed with oil, that they may be as living stones enlivened by the Spirit and cemented together with love. We pray to the Lord.

**7.** (Add your group petition.)

**Leader:** God of power,
    you give us the oil of salvation
    to transform us into the likeness of Christ
        your Son.
Hear the prayers we offer with all our
        hearts,
    and never abandon the people who share
        your life.
We ask this through Christ our Lord.

**R/.** Amen.

## Lord's Prayer

**Leader:** Gathered as one body in Christ, let us pray in the words that Jesus gave us:

**All:** Our Father . . . .

## CONCLUSION

**Leader:** Let us pray: (*Silence*)

God of mercy and love,
from the fruit of the olive tree
you give us the oil for holy chrism,
and through this sign,
you give us your life and love.
Open our hearts to be transformed
into the likeness of Christ your Son
so that we may share in his royal,
priestly, and prophetic work.
We ask this through Christ our Lord.

**R/.** Amen.

**Leader:** (*Concludes by signing himself or herself with the sign of the cross and saying:*)
    May God the Father, with the Son and the Holy Spirit, be praised and blessed for ever and ever.

**R/.** Amen.

*W*hen you hear the word *oil*, what images, experiences, aromas, tastes, or physical properties come to mind?

**With a partner, list 5 responses in the next three minutes. (You may surprise yourself and come up with more than 5 items in this brief brainstorming session.) Share your lists.**

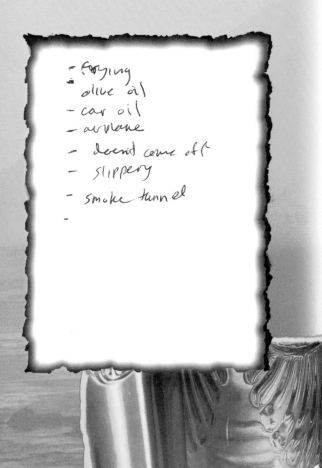

- frying
- olive oil
- car oil
- airplane
- doesn't come off
- slippery
- smoke tunnel
-

## A Precious Commodity

Oil is so common in our lives that we rarely give it a thought. Only when we start to list its uses do we realize how much we depend on this substance. Look at some of the uses you listed:

- cooking oil for moistening, and flavoring;

- polishing oil for preserving wood furniture and floors;

- baby oil, beauty oil, and suntan oils for moisturing and protecting skin;

- nutritional oil for eliminating impurities, preserving skin and hair;

- medicinal oil for limbering muscles, treating wounds, promoting healing.

The value and importance of oil is not a modern discovery. Its significance to the human race goes back thousands and thousands of years. From very early times oil was used for lighting, for nourishment, for healing, for soothing. Oil became so essential to human development that it is safe to say that, without it, life in ancient times would not have been possible.

No wonder, then, that what had become so precious in the preservation and development of physical life would also become a profound expression of spiritual realities as well.

# Chosen and Anointed

In the Old Testament we find many incidents involving anointing with oil. Oil is a sign of abundance and joy; it relaxes and cleanses; it soothes and "makes radiant with beauty, health, and strength" (*Catechism,* 1293.) That is why oil was used to anoint the kings, prophets, and priests who were chosen by God to lead and guide the people. The oil symbolized God's desire to bless, heal, and consecrate, or set apart for a sacred work. Anointing with oil signified that God would be with that person in a special way.

Do you remember the story of David, the young shepherd of Bethlehem? It is told in 1 Samuel 16:1–13. Saul, the first king of Israel, has been rejected by God because he has turned away from God's law. The Lord tells the prophet Samuel to ignore Saul and to go instead to a man in Bethlehem called Jesse who has many sons. The Lord tells Samuel that he has chosen one of them to be king in Saul's place.

So Samuel went to Bethlehem and met with Jesse and seven of his sons.

Jesse introduced his sons to Samuel but the Lord rejected each one, telling the prophet that appearances are not what counts; he must look at the heart.

Finally Samuel asked Jesse if he had any more sons. Jesse replied that his youngest son, David, was out in the fields tending the sheep. "Send for him," Samuel said. Jesse sent for David and the young man came and stood before Samuel.

The LORD said, "There—anoint him, for this is he!" Then Samuel, with the horn of oil in hand, anointed him in the midst of his brothers; and from that day on, the spirit of the LORD rushed upon David.

David was faithful to God's call and, filled with wisdom and courage, became a great king. He wasn't perfect, of course, but the Spirit of God helped him to use his gifts and talents in God's service. It is not by chance that David became the ancestor of Jesus, the promised Messiah.

**An Arab shepherd tends his flock outside Bethlehem.**

49

Let's pause for a minute and reflect on this Scripture story. Sit as quietly as you can; breathe deeply and slowly. Try to become aware of the Spirit of God who is with you and within you. Listen as the story is read again.

Imagine you are David. You are out in the fields taking care of your father's flock. As the youngest in the family you probably get the chores that your older brothers don't want! You spend your days protecting the sheep from dangers, especially predators. (You even killed a mountain lion once!) During quieter moments you make up songs and play them on your harp (an ancestor of the guitar).

One day out of the blue you are summoned home by your father and presented to the great prophet Samuel. Samuel pours oil on your head; you can feel it in your hair and streaming down your face. The prophet announces that God has chosen you to be king of Israel!

What is your reaction as Samuel anoints you with oil? Do you understand right away what is happening? What do you feel as the Spirit of God "rushes in on you"?

No wonder that the Church treasures this story from sacred Scripture! How clearly it reminds us of the significance of holy oil is as a sacramental sign in the Church.

*Recognizing that you will soon be anointed with holy oil in Confirmation, take a moment now to tell God what it means to you to be chosen by God for his service. Write your prayer here.*

> The anointing with oil symbolizes that hard, honest, work was worth it. For this, God has chosen me.

**Symbol TALK**

*Anointing with oil* signifies the presence of the Holy Spirit. It is the sacramental sign of Confirmation, the second sacrament of initiation. Anointing with chrism, together with the laying on of hands, communicates the Gift of the Spirit and the indelible seal of Jesus on the one he has chosen as his follower.

At the Chrism Mass the bishop also blesses two other holy oils. The *oil of the sick* is used in the sacrament of Anointing of the Sick. The *oil of catechumens* is used in the early stages of a catechumen's preparation for the sacraments of initiation at the Easter Vigil.

## A Sign of the Spirit

Down through the ages the Church has continued this tradition of anointing with fragrant oil as a sign of blessing, healing, and consecration. Oil is so closely identified with the Gift of the Spirit that it is considered a sign of the Spirit's presence. In confirming you the bishop will place his right hand on your head and with his thumb he will anoint your forehead with the sign of the cross saying, "Be sealed with the Gift of the Holy Spirit." At that moment the Holy Spirit will "rush" upon you just as it did upon the apostles at Pentecost.

Anointing with oil is the essential sacramental sign of Confirmation. By this anointing you will receive the indelible "mark," the seal of the Holy Spirit. The seal of the Holy Spirit marks you as belonging completely to Christ and as one who shares fully in his mission.

The oil used in Confirmation is called *chrism*. *Chrism* is a fragrant oil extracted from olives and mixed with balm. It is consecrated by the bishop at a Chrism Mass during Holy Week. The bishop blesses the oil by extending his hands and praying that the anointing with oil will bring strength and abundance of joy. He concludes:

> Father, by the power of your love,
> make this mixture of oil and perfume
> a sign and source † of your blessing.
> Pour out the gifts of your Holy Spirit
> on our brothers and sisters who will be
> anointed with it.
> Let the splendor of holiness shine on the world
> from every place and thing
> signed with this oil.

*The Blessing of Oils and Chrism*

The anointing with chrism at Confirmation is the sacramental sign that the Holy Spirit is upon us, helping us to be faithful disciples and empowering us to share more fully in the mission of Jesus Christ. This seal of the Spirit, however, is not magic; it is not automatic. It requires our cooperation, our willingness to follow Christ and to accept the responsibilities of discipleship.

*Just as with David, your anointing comes with both gifts and responsibilities. We talked about the gifts; what do you think are the responsibilities of someone sealed with the Gift of the Spirit?*

## In the Likeness of Christ

If you come to Confirmation with faith and an open heart, the seal of the Spirit will transform you; it will help you become more like Jesus, to be transformed in his likeness. You will understand in a deeper way that Jesus has chosen you to belong to him totally, to be his disciple for ever. The Holy Spirit will encourage you to grow in your Catholic faith, to become a true Christian (anointed one), willing and prepared to witness to Christ. As a member of the Church, you belong to a priestly and prophetic people, bringing to others the love of God and the good news and making the divine life in you visible in your service of others. What will this require of you as a young Catholic in today's world?

### Key Words

**chrism:** a perfumed oil consecrated by the bishop during Holy Week and used in anointing those who are being baptized, confirmed, or consecrated in Holy Orders

**Christ:** the Anointed One, the Messiah, from the Greek word for "anointed one"

## REALITY CHECK
### (Be specific!)

| Christ was: | Times when I need to be more like Christ: |
|---|---|
| COMPASSIONATE | Show caring & love to people that I have been neglecting. |
| MERCIFUL | I should forgive people before seeking forgiveness. |
| FORGIVING | ↓ |
| FAITHFUL | Be excited about my faith. Always find hope. |
| RESPECTFUL | Respect my friends, neighbors, environment, surroundings. |
| JUST | Seek fairness in all decisions I make |

# The Pope & YOUth

Pope John Paul II calls you and all believers to accept the Gift of the Spirit we receive in Baptism and Confirmation and to put its effects to work in the world.

Baptism and Confirmation do not remove us from the world, for we share the joys and hopes of people today. . . . Thanks to Christ we are close to all our brothers and sisters, and we are called to show the profound joy, which is found in living with him. The Lord calls us to undertake our mission right where we are. . . . Whatever we do, our existence is for the Lord: That is our hope and our title to glory.

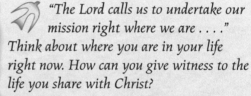 *"The Lord calls us to undertake our mission right where we are . . . ."* Think about where you are in your life right now. How can you give witness to the life you share with Christ?

# MAPPING

## POINTS OF DEPARTURE

Name one issue that confronts you today and how the Gift of the Spirit can help you meet that challenge.

### SYMBOLS ON THE MAP

What meaning is communicated by the symbol of anointing with oil?

## Destination Points

Let's discuss:

We are Christians, anointed ones. What effect should that have on the way we live?

# THE JOURNEY

## JOURNAL NOTES

### Reflections

Pope John Paul II challenges each of us to accept the Gift of the Spirit and to put its effects to work in the world.

### My Prayer:

Holy Spirit, I want to accept the challenge and to use my gifts to

## closing Prayer

God of mercy and love,
from the fruit of the olive tree
you give us the oil for holy chrism,
and through this sign,
you give us your life and love.
Open our hearts to be transformed
into the likeness of Christ your Son
so that we may share in his royal, priestly,
and prophetic work.
Amen.

# More Like Christ

I am the vine, you are the branches.
Whoever remains in me and I in him
will bear much fruit, because
without me you can do nothing.

John 15:5

# OPENING PRAYER

**Entrance Song:** *(Use the entrance song that will be sung at Confirmation.)*

**Leader:** In the name of the Father, and of the Son, and of the Holy Spirit.

**R/.** Amen.

**Leader:** Brothers and sisters, give praise to God, who sends us the Holy Spirit to live in our hearts and has favored us in wonderful ways. Blessed be God now and for ever.

**R/.** Amen.

**Leader:** Let us pray. *(Silence)*

O gracious Father,
your Son gave us the new commandment:
"Love one another as I have loved you."
Help us to understand what it means
to love one another and to live as Christ's
followers in this world.

Give us your Spirit
so that we may find true joy
as a people who are anointed

into the life of Christ
and enrolled in his service for ever.

We ask this through Christ our Lord.

**R/.** Amen.

### LITURGY OF THE WORD

**Reading:** Ephesians 1:3–14

**Responsorial Psalm:** *(Use the responsorial psalm that will be sung at Confirmation.)*

**Gospel Acclamation:** *(Use the acclamation that will be sung at Confirmation.)*

**Gospel:** John 15:14–17

**Reflection**

### HONORING THE CROSS

**Leader:** God has made the cross of Christ the sign of our salvation for through his death on the cross we have been given new life.
At our Baptism the sign of the cross was imprinted on our bodies

so that we might always walk in the
footsteps of Christ,
and it is through this sign that we are
reminded of what it means
to live like Christ in this world.
Come forward now and honor the cross,
which we embraced at our Baptism.

*(All come forward to honor the cross using an
appropriate sign of reverence, for example, a bow, touch,
kiss. An appropriate song or background music is played
during this procession.)*

## General Intercessions

Leader: As we journey on the path that leads to
the kingdom, let us pray for the needs of the
Church. Our response is: *Lord, hear our prayer.*

**1.** That we, your Church, may have *wisdom* to
depend on God for all our needs. We pray to the
Lord.

**2.** That we, your baptized ones, may have
*understanding* of the sorrows and joys of all God's
people. We pray to the Lord.

**3.** That we, your followers, may practice *reverence,*
respecting others and avoiding all forms of
violence. We pray to the Lord.

**4.** That we, soon to be confirmed Catholics, may
have *courage* to work for justice for all peoples
and to change unjust conditions in this world.
We pray to the Lord.

**5.** That we, your disciples, may practice *right
judgment* so as to overcome all anger and let
compassion rule our lives.
We pray to the Lord.

**6.** That we, your chosen ones, may have the
*knowledge* to choose only what is right and good
and to be faithful on our journey of salvation.
We pray to the Lord.

**7.** That we, your anointed ones, may show *wonder
and awe* at the diversity of all peoples and cultures
so as to build a world of peace. We pray to the Lord.

**8.** (Add your group petition.)

Leader: God of love,
your will for us is that we live joined to Christ
as branches are joined to the vine.
Hear the prayers we offer with all our hearts,
and never abandon those who share your life.

R/. Amen.

## LORDS PRAYER

Leader: Gathered as one body in Christ, let us
pray in the words that Jesus gave us:

All: Our Father . . . .

## CONCLUSION

Leader: Let us pray. *(Silence)*

Almighty and eternal God,
may we who participate in the mystery
of the cross
never cease to live this sign in our lives.
Through the seal of the Holy Spirit
we are anointed in the image of Christ.
Lead us to a profound understanding
of what it means to be marked as
Christ's witnesses in this world.

We ask this through Christ our Lord.

R/. Amen.

Leader: *(Concludes by signing himself or herself
with the sign of the cross and saying:)*
May God the Father, with the Son and the Holy
Spirit, be praised and blessed for ever and ever.

R/. Amen.

*I am the vine,
you are the branches.
Whoever remains in me
and I in him
will bear much fruit,
because without me
you can do nothing.*
**John 15:5**

**What a powerful image! We are united to Jesus, joined to him, so that his very life flows through us. Jesus says: "Remain in my love" (John 15:9). How do we do that? Read John 15:10 to see what Jesus meant.**

## I Call You Friends

For the disciples these words of Jesus must have been truly amazing: "I no longer call you slaves . . . I have called you friends" (John 15:15). They knew that all the great figures of the Old Testament, including Moses and David, had been called "servants" or "slaves of Yahweh." Only Abraham had been called a "friend of God." And now Jesus was giving them this great honor, this great gift: "You are my friends" (John 15:14).

This friendship depends on one big "if," however. "If," Jesus says, "you do what I command you." Our relationship with Christ, our friendship with him, is based on one thing: "This I command you: love one another" (John 15:17).

How simple this seems! How easily we say these words. Then we try to put them into practice and discover the reality. The love Jesus asks for is not sentimental, not romantic, not just a pleasant feeling. It is the kind of love that goes beyond outward appearances and attitudes to see, as God told Samuel before anointing David, "what is in the heart."

We see this kind of love in parents, for example, who tenderly care for their children in good times and in bad. True friends show this love as well when they give support unconditionally, not because they feel obliged, but because they wish to. We see this love in those who care for and serve the sick, the poor, the outcasts—not because they will be rewarded, but because they realize that this is the kind of love Jesus was talking about when he said, "Love one another."

Love one another. "What do you mean, Jesus? Do you mean, I'm supposed to love the unlovable? The people who don't love me back? The people who are unpleasant, even obnoxious? The people who are unattractive in looks and behavior? You don't mean these people, do you, Lord?

The words of Jesus are clear and unambiguous: "This I command you: love one another."

If we accept Jesus' offer of friendship with him, we must accept his command to love—even when, or maybe *especially* when, it is hard. This is how we "remain" with Jesus. This is what it means to be his disciple. If you were listening carefully to the gospel reading in today's prayer then you heard what Jesus promised his friends: "I have told you this so that my joy might be in you and your joy might be complete" (John 15:11).

We, then, as committed Catholics live as friends and disciples of Jesus when we love others as he asks—not with a "have to" mentality, but freely, generously, expecting nothing in return but the complete joy Jesus promises us.

*Whenever you are unhappy or afraid or anxious or unsure about the love of others, call to mind the words of Jesus: "I call you friend." Why not put these words where you can see them easily each day? Describe how you will do this.*

# Discipleship

How do we become disciples of Jesus Christ? Jesus showed us the way. He wanted to be with us for all time and so he gave us the Church. It is through membership in the Church that we become disciples of Jesus. A disciple of Jesus is one who follows him and learns from him.

As disciples of Jesus we try to become like the one we follow. We know that Jesus is the Son of God and our Savior who, in the mystery of the incarnation, became one of us. Christians describe the *incarnation* as the union of divinity with humanity in Jesus Christ. It is the mystery of Jesus Christ being God and Man. Jesus is the Word of God made flesh. He became one of us in all things except sin. The Church teaches that Jesus *was truly* a man. He was not God in human disguise.

What was Jesus like as one of us? What did he try to tell us about God? The gospels do not provide us with everything there is to know about Jesus but they do give us an idea of what kind of an individual he was.

During his life on earth he certainly made many friends—and enemies, too. But it is clear that both friends and foes saw him as a compelling and impressive man. Here was one who knew who he was and what life was all about. Those who heard and saw him were amazed. They said, "Never before has anyone spoken like this one" (John 7:46).

People were drawn to him—and it seems he was drawn to them in return. He went to their homes and ate with them; he reached out to them in the marketplace, in the streets, in the workplace. He went to their weddings—and their funerals. He did not keep his distance but was truly involved in the lives of people.

He was a friend; he shared himself with others. He rejoiced with his friends when things were going well; he wept with them when they were sad. No one was a stranger in his eyes—the rich, the poor, the young and the old, the one who obeyed the law and the sinner—all were accepted by him and felt comfortable with him.

Jesus went out of his way for those who were sick or rejected by others. It was clear that Jesus was no weakling. Discouraged and rejected at times, he never gave up. Hated and spurned, he loved in return. Like us, he had moments of anger and loneliness, too. Misunderstood by many—even his disciples—he never changed what he knew he had to do and say. He found comfort and strength in God his Father and frequently went off alone to be with his Father in prayer.

In the end, of course, he showed us what real love is all about by giving his life for all of us. "No one has greater love than this, to lay down one's life for one's friends" (John 15:13). The gospels, then, show us a strong, warm, loving, focused man—fully alive and fully human. This is the Christ we follow. This is the one in whose service we are enrolled.

 *What attracts you to Christ? In what ways would you like to be more like him?*

Denver Youth Day with the Holy Father

## True Witnesses

Just like the apostles who first heard Christ's new commandment, and the early Church who received the words from them, we, too, are his disciples.

One way to describe a disciple is to say it is someone who takes a chance with Jesus. This was certainly true of the first disciples of Jesus who at his word left everything to follow him. In turn, Jesus takes a chance with us; he puts the whole future of the Church into our hands. What an overwhelming thought: Jesus puts the gospel in our hands and tells us to do something with it. The gospel is not something private, something just for ourselves that we can store away untouched. The good news of Christ must be shared, spread, proclaimed, lived.

A famous teacher of the early Church, Saint John Chrysostom, challenged his Christian community to live their discipleship before an unbelieving world in this way: He said, "Let us, before all words, astound them by our way of life."

What do we mean by a Christian way of life? It is a moral life, a life of faith in Christ. It means that we:

• take on the attitude of Christ, aided by God's grace, seeing the connection between the new life in the Spirit and the moral life

• recognize God as our Father, seeing one another as brothers and sisters

• grow in the knowledge of our faith, especially the Beatitudes and the Ten Commandments

• avoid the evil of sin— thoughts, words, and deeds, contrary to God's law

• understand the importance of the virtues

• recognize the power of grace

• regularly pray and celebrate the sacraments

You must never underestimate the Gift of the Holy Spirit in your life. It is the Spirit who is at work in and through you. Every time you do what you know is good, every time you are kind to another, every time you are compassionate and forgiving, you make a difference. You make Christ present to another—and that is astounding!

The Christian moral life must be grounded in and supported by prayer. The *Catechism* defines prayer as "the raising of one's mind and heart to God or the requesting of good things from God" (2590). It is the Holy Spirit who makes it possible for us to pray. Besides times of personal prayer, the Church provides many opportunities for communal prayer, especially in the liturgy and on the feasts of the liturgical year.

Take a minute now to pray together the words of the closing prayer of the opening rite beginning: "Almighty and eternal God . . ."

# The Pope & YOUth

In 1999 the Holy Father challenged the young people in St. Louis:

"You are the light of the world . . . ."

Dear Young People,

Ask yourselves: Do I believe these words of Jesus in the gospel? Jesus is calling you the light of the world. He is asking you to let your light shine before others. I know that in your hearts you want to say: "Here I am, Lord. Here I am. I come to do your will." But only if you are one with Jesus can you share his light and be a light to the world.

Are you ready for this?

Because Jesus is the Light, we, too, become light when we proclaim him. This is the heart of the Christian mission to which each of you are called through Baptism and Confirmation. You are called to make the light of Christ shine brightly in the world.

*What are some of the "darknesses" in yourself that need the light of Christ? What things or issues in the world are still dark, still without his light?*

## POINTS OF DEPARTURE

"Whoever remains in me and I in him will bear much fruit, because without me you can do nothing" (John 15:5).

How does a confirmed Catholic "remain" in Christ?

**SYMBOLS ON THE MAP**

How will you be marked with the sign of the cross at Confirmation?

## Destination Points

Let's discuss:

Who is Jesus for you?

# THE JOURNEY

## JOURNAL NOTES

**Reflection**

Jesus calls me to be his disciple. I live this out in the way I love others with no strings attached.

*My Prayer:*

Holy Spirit, I know I'm expected to love everyone just as you love me. When I find it hard, please

## closing *Prayer*

God our Father,
complete the work you have begun
and keep the gifts of your Holy Spirit
active in the hearts of your people.
Make them ready to live his Gospel
and eager to do his will.
May they never be ashamed
to proclaim to all the world
    Christ crucified
living and reigning for ever and ever.
Amen.

*The Rite of Confirmation*

# In the Unity
# of Faith

You feed your people
and strengthen them in holiness,
so that the family of mankind
may come to walk in the light
of one faith
in one communion of love.

Sacramentary

# ～ OPENING PRAYER ～

**Entrance Song:** *(Use the entrance song that will be sung at Confirmation.)*

**Leader:** In the name of the Father, and of the Son, and of the Holy Spirit.

**R/. Amen.**

**Leader:** *(greets those present in the following words)*

Brothers and sisters, give praise to God, who sends us the Holy Spirit to live in our hearts and has favored us in wonderful ways. Blessed be God now and for ever.

**R/. Amen.**

**Leader:** Let us pray. *(Silence)*

O loving God,
through Baptism you make us one family in
   Christ your Son,
one in the communion of his Spirit,
and one in the sharing of his Body and Blood.
Help us to grow in love for one another
and walk in the unity of faith as the
   body of Christ
so that we may be his witnesses to the ends
   of the earth.

We ask this through Christ our Lord.

**R/. Amen.**

## LITURGY OF THE WORD

**Reading:** Acts 1:3–8

**Responsorial Psalm:** *(Use the responsorial psalm that will be sung at Confirmation.)*

**Gospel Acclamation:** *Use the acclamation that will be sung at Confirmation.)*

**Gospel:** John 6:44–57

**Reflection**

### General Intercessions

**Leader:** As we walk in the unity of faith, let us pray for all those who give witness to their life in Christ. Our response is *Lord, hear our prayer.*

**1.** For those who witness Christ to those who have never heard the good news, that they may have the gift of *wisdom* to make Christ known in this world. We pray to the Lord.

**2.** For those who witness Christ to those who are alienated and exploited in this world, that they may have the gift of *courage* to stand up to oppression and discrimination. We pray to the Lord.

70

**3.** For those who witness Christ to the hungry and the poor, that they may have the gift of *understanding* the needs of God's children. We pray to the Lord.

**4.** For those who witness Christ to the ill and dying, that they may have the gift of *reverence* for the dignity of those they serve. We pray to the Lord.

**5.** For those who witness Christ to the imprisoned, that they may have the gift of *right judgment* to meet the needs of those who seek justice and forgiveness. We pray to the Lord.

**6.** For those who witness Christ to refugees and immigrants, that they may have the gift of *knowledge* to appreciate the different cultures and nations of our world. We pray to the Lord.

**7.** For those who witness Christ to those broken in heart, mind and spirit, that they may have the gifts of *wonder and awe* to see the face of Christ in each person they meet. We pray to the Lord.

**8.** (Add your group petition.)

**Leader:** Almighty, everliving God,
your will for us is that we remain faithful
    to you
throughout the days of our lives.
Hear the prayers of your people,
who witness your presence in this world.

R/. Amen.

**Lord's Prayer**

**Leader:** Gathered as one body in Christ, let us pray in the words that Jesus gave us:

**All:** Our Father . . . .

**Sign of Peace**

**Leader:** As one body in Christ,
let us offer one another the sign of
    unity and peace.

## CONCLUSION

**Leader:** Let us pray. *(Silence)*

Almighty and eternal God,
we proclaim one Lord, one faith,
    one Baptism.
Through the Gift of your Spirit
strenghen us in the unity of our faith
that we may bear witness to Christ
for the building up of his body in faith
    and love.

We ask this through Christ our Lord.

R/. Amen.

**Leader:** *(Concludes by signing himself or herself with the sign of the cross and saying:)*

May God the Father, with the Son and the Holy Spirit, be praised and blessed for ever and ever.

R/. Amen.

Certain peoples of Zimbabwe in southern Africa greet each other by saying, "How are you?" The response is, "I am well if you are well." The first person then says, "I am well so we are well."

**What does this exchange tell us about the culture of the people? What one word or phrase can you think of to describe what this simple greeting is all about?**

## We Are the Church

What about us? Are we so aware of our connection with one another, our unity in the Church that we can truly say that our well-being is connected to the well-being of another? "I am well if you are well." "I am well so we are well."

We live in a society in which business, technology, and the media make it easy for people to be separate from one another. Sometimes neighbors do not even know one another, let alone rely on one another for help.

In a faith community, we cannot live in isolation. Jesus called us together to be one body, the Church. We depend on one another just as each part of a body depends on another part. We belong to the universal body of Christ and every part of that body is mutually dependent. Saint Paul explained this to the first Christians saying:

"The eye cannot say to the hand, 'I do not need you,' nor again the head to the feet, 'I do not need you.'"

1 Corinthians 12:21

This unity we share in the Church begins at the very moment of our Baptism. The celebrant prays to God the Father:

> From all who are baptized in water and the
> Holy Spirit,
> you have formed one people,
> united in your Son, Jesus Christ.

*Rite of Baptism*

Our unity is deepened and strengthened in Confirmation. But Confirmation is not the end of our growth in Christ: it moves us toward the Sacrament of sacraments, the Eucharist. Eucharist completes Christian initiation into the Church. Those who become God's adopted children at Baptism and are further transformed into the likeness of Christ at Confirmation, now share with the whole Catholic community in Jesus' life, death, and resurrection through the Eucharist.

*Read again the opening prayer on page 70. Underline the words that tell of the unity, the oneness we share through the sacraments of initiation. Write the key words here.*

Baptism: one ___Family in Christ___

___

Confirmation: one ___in the communion___

___of his spirit___

Eucharist: one ___in the sharing___

___of His body and blood___

### Key Words

**covenant (biblical):** a solemn agreement between God and his people, legally binding on both sides and confirmed by offering a sacrifice to God or by a solemn ritual

**Communion:** another name for the Eucharist, the Body and Blood of Christ; the sign and source of our reconciliation and union with God and one another

**Eucharist:** the sacrament of the Body and Blood of Christ, who is truly present—body, blood, soul, and divinity—under the appearances of bread and wine

**Liturgy:** the official public prayer of the Church in which we proclaim and celebrate the mystery of Christ

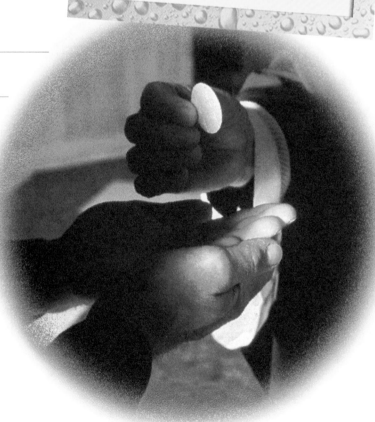

The Supper at Emmaus, *Diego Velázquez, 1599–1660*

## The Sacrament of Sacraments

At the Last Supper the night before he died, Jesus instituted the Eucharist, the sacrament of his Body and Blood. He did this so that the saving power of his sacrifice on the cross might continue throughout the ages. The Eucharist is the memorial of Jesus' death and resurrection. It is not a memorial in stone or marble but a living re-presentation of Christ's saving acts. We hear of his sacrifice in the very words Christ used when he instituted the Eucharist: "This is my body, which will be given for you. . . . This cup is the new covenant in my blood, which will be shed for you" (Luke 22:19–20). The Eucharist is a memorial that calls the Church together to participate in Christ's sacrifice, to worship as one people—a living sign of unity in the bond of love.

The Eucharist is also a sacred meal in which we come to the table of the Lord to partake in the Body and Blood of Christ under the appearances of bread and wine. We do not do this in isolation but as a worshiping community.

Down through the ages at every Mass the mystery of the Eucharist is continued: Christ offers himself as a sacrifice for us and we are united to him and to one another in a holy meal. The Eucharist, therefore, lies at the heart of the Church's life and is its high point.

## A Sign of Unity

In the early days of the Church, The Eucharist was the center of a larger meal to which people were to bring food to share—and a surplus to be shared with the poor. The Christians of Corinth forgot that the Eucharist is a sign of unity. They forgot that we are to be one, not only with Jesus, but with one another, so that we can share his life with the world. They celebrated the Eucharist while ignoring the poor and needy. Saint Paul reminded them that those who *receive* the Eucharist must be willing to *give* the Eucharist—the Bread that is broken must be shared. Paul made it clear that the purpose of their gathering for Eucharist was to unite them to Christ and to one another. "Because the loaf of bread is one," Paul wrote to the Corinthians, "we, though many, are one body, for we all partake of the one loaf." (1 Corinthians 10:17).

As you prepare for Confirmation it is important that you reflect once again on the meaning of Eucharist. Unlike Baptism and Confirmation which can be received only once, we are encouraged to come to the table of the Lord as frequently as possible. Why? Because each time we receive Christ in Holy Communion we are nourished and strengthened to continue his work in the world. The word *Mass* means "to be sent forth;" *we* are sent forth from the Eucharist to live as Jesus did, to share his love with others, and to serve the needs of our brothers and sisters in the world.

*Imagine: What would the world be like if every Catholic who received the Eucharist began to live as Jesus did? What about you? What might change in your family life? In your dealings with others? In the way you see the world around you? Would your list of priorities change? Write your thoughts here.*

*Family life would be peaceful, full of love and joy.
Dealings with others would be healthy and selfless*

## Symbol TALK

**The Breaking of Bread:**
At the Last Supper Jesus took bread and broke it. He gave it to the disciples saying, "This is my body". . . (Luke 22:19). From the earliest days of the Church this symbolic action of breaking bread was the name the first Christians gave their Eucharistic assemblies. What today we call the Mass, they called the Breaking of Bread because this action symbolized that all who eat the one broken bread—Christ—become united to him and form one body in him.

Just before Holy Communion at Mass we see the priest break the host into pieces. What does this mean? It means that Jesus is the one Bread of Life broken and shared among us. When we receive Holy Communion we do not receive many Christs—we receive the one Body of Christ broken for us.

*Read the story of the disciples on the road to Emmaus (Luke 24:13–35). At what point do the disciples recognize Jesus?*

## Walk in the Unity of Faith

Sometimes Catholics think that Confirmation is like a graduation, marking the end of a time of growing up, of formation. Now they may feel that they have nothing more to learn about their faith; they have "arrived" and their growing time is complete.

Not so! The truth is that Confirmation opens up *new* challenges to us on our journey of faith. We are challenged to become more like Christ; we are challenged to pray, study, and use our gifts to make the world a better place. We are challenged to deepen our understanding of the gospel message and to measure the issues of our world against that message.

The Church helps us. Guided by the Holy Spirit, the Church passes on the word of God as found in Scripture and the Church's living tradition. The Church continually confronts the issues of our time applying in every age the sacred deposit of faith as found in Scripture and tradition. This is done frequently through the encyclicals (letters) of the popes and the pastoral letters of our bishops. Here is what the Church teaches about some of these important issues:

- *racism* The bishops of the United States have reminded us that racial prejudice is a sin. It has no place in the life of any Catholic. Each person must be treated with dignity and respect as a son or daughter of God. We are all brothers and sisters in Christ.

- *war and peace* Ours is a fragile world. We must work for a peace that is based on justice and freedom and eradicate the senseless race to build and to spread weapons of war.

- *economic justice* Each human person must be given the chance to work for the basic necessities of life. An obsession for wealth at the expense of others' lives is one of the greatest social sins of our time.

- *abortion and euthanasia* All life is sacred; all life belongs to God. Deliberate destruction of life through abortion or euthanasia is a serious sin against God's law.

- *capital punishment* Increasingly, followers of Christ are recognizing that the dignity of human life must never be taken away, even in the case of someone who has done great evil. The Church encourages people to turn away from the ineffective solution of the death penalty and to begin the more difficult task of building peace in our troubled society.

On these issues and others, such as sexism, ageism, consumerism, and environmental concerns, the leaders of our Church have helped us to see and to apply the teachings of Jesus Christ to the complicated problems that face us. This is how we are called to make a difference in our world.

Jesus has invited us to follow him, to walk in his footsteps, to complete his mission on earth. To do this we must reach out to others as he did with care, concern, healing and hope. This is a *way of life* for a confirmed Catholic.

*Think of a serious moral issue that is prevalent in your world. It might be drug abuse, sexual promiscuity, alcoholism, stealing, or violence, for example. Describe it. How do you respond to it as a follower of Jesus Christ?*

## The Church & YOUth

What does Confirmation have to do with the Eucharist? Why is this sacrament usually celebrated during the liturgy of the Mass?

The Eucharist is the center and the summit of Catholic life. Both Baptism and Confirmation, which are so closely related, lead us to the table of the Lord. It is here that we are nourished by the Bread of Life to live out our public witness to Jesus Christ. In celebrating the Eucharist, we demonstrate our *yes* to being confirmed in the Spirit of Christ. Filled with the Spirit in Confirmation we recommit ourselves to come to the Eucharist to worship with our parish community, and to go forth from the Eucharist to love and serve others in Jesus' name.

*Jesus asks you now to be his hands, his eyes, his voice, his heart in the world. How will you answer him?*

How are these young people responding to the invitation to walk in the footsteps of Jesus?

## POINTS OF DEPARTURE

Why is the Eucharist called "the Sacrament of sacraments"?

What is the significance of the "breaking of bread" in the Eucharist?

## Destination Points

Let's discuss:

How will you show in your daily life that you have accepted your responsibility as a confirmed Catholic?

# THE JOURNEY

*Reflections*

The message is loud and clear.
Be a witness for Christ.

*My Prayer:*

Holy Spirit, the challenges I face to do this are real.
The biggest ones for me are:




Holy Spirit, thank you for



closing *Prayer*

Loving Father,
you give your Son as food
to those you anoint with your Spirit.
Help them to fulfill your law
by living in freedom as your children.
May they live in holiness
and be your witnesses to the world.

*The Rite of Confirmation*

# Confirmation Retreat

**Theme  The Holy Spirit—Giver of Life**

The Holy Spirit is called the Lord and *Giver of Life*. We call the Holy Spirit the Giver of life because we share in the divine life through the power of the Holy Spirit. We often express this truth by saying that we are temples of the Holy Spirit.

## Introduction

Today is a retreat day for you in preparation for receiving the sacrament of Confirmation. A retreat is a very special time for prayer and reflection. Did it ever occur to you that Jesus, too, made retreats? In the gospels we read that Jesus often went apart to pray, sometimes alone and other times with his disciples. People usually make retreats just before making a big decision or beginning a new endeavor.

As in all of life, it takes hard work to succeed. For example, athletes and musicians practice day in and day out, hour after hour, to become the best. It takes commitment and determined effort to achieve success. Sometimes we forget that it takes hard work to live a good life. The Church is inviting you to commit yourself to working hard at being a witness for Christ today in our world. The Church needs you to become your best self as a true follower of Christ.

Two key questions to ask yourself during this retreat are:

❖ What does the sacrament of Confirmation mean to me?

❖ How can this sacrament help me to make right choices, to choose good over evil, to live more consistently the gospel values that Jesus came to teach us?

# Morning Praise

**Opening Hymn**

Leader: Let us pray together:

All: In the name of the Father, and of the Son, and of the Holy Spirit. Amen.

## Gathering Prayer

All: Come Holy Spirit, fill the hearts of your faithful and kindle in them the fire of your love.

Leader: Send forth your Spirit and they shall be created

All: And you will renew the face of the earth.

Leader: Let us pray.

All: Lord, by the light of the Holy Spirit, you have taught the hearts of the faithful. In the same Spirit help us to relish what is right and always rejoice in your consolation.
We ask this through Christ our Lord. Amen.

Reader: A reading from the Gospel of John, chapter 14, verses 15 to 31.

All: Thanks be to God.

Reflection: In this reading we heard the words:
"Peace I leave with you; my peace I give to you. Do not let your hearts be troubled or afraid."

Take a few minutes and ask yourself: Am I at peace with myself? Are there some things that cause me to be anxious or afraid? How can the sacrament of Confirmation help me to be at peace and to overcome my fears and anxieties?

Journal your thoughts and prayers about these questions.

Leader: Let us pray together Psalm 121.

**Side 1:** I raise my eyes toward the mountains.
    From where will my help come?

**Side 2:** My help comes from the LORD,
    the maker of heaven and earth.

**Side 1:** God will not allow your foot to slip;
    your guardian does not sleep.

**Side 2:** Truly, the guardian of Israel
    never slumbers nor sleeps.

**Side 1:** The LORD is your guardian;
    the LORD is your shade
    at your right hand.

**Side 2:** By day the sun cannot harm you,
    nor the moon by night.

**Side 1:** The LORD will guard you from all evil,
    will always guard your life.

**All:** The LORD will guard your coming and going
    both now and forever.

**All:** Glory be to the Father . . . .

**Leader:** A reading from the Gospel of Luke, chapter 11, verse 1.

He was praying in a certain place, and when he had finished, one of his
    disciples said to him,

**All:** "Lord, teach us to pray just as John taught his disciples."

**Leader:** Let us pray the Our Father in the words we use at Mass:

**All:** Our Father . . . .

## Reflection

Have you ever asked Jesus to teach you to pray?
Take a few minutes now and think about this and all the things you prayed
for in the Our Father. Quietly offer your own prayer to God the Father,
through Jesus, his Son, in the unity of the Holy Spirit.

## Closing Prayer

All: God, our Father, let your Spirit come upon us with power to fill us with
his gifts. May the Spirit make our hearts pleasing to you and ready to do
your will. We ask this through our Lord Jesus Christ, your Son, who lives
and reigns with you and the Holy Spirit, one God, for ever and ever.
Amen.

## First Conference: Acts 1:8

*"You will receive power when the holy Spirit comes upon you, and you will be my
witnesses in Jerusalem, throughout Judea and Samaria, and to the ends of the earth."*

## Ritual and Renewal of Baptismal Promises

Leader: I invite you now to renew the promises of Baptism that were
made for you at the time of your Baptism.

Leader: Do you reject Satan and all his works and all his empty promises?

All: I do.

Leader: Do you believe in God the Father almighty, creator
of heaven and earth?

All: I do.

Leader: Do you believe in Jesus Christ, his only Son, our Lord,
who was born of the Virgin Mary, was crucified, died, and was buried,
rose from the dead, and is now seated at the right hand of the Father?

All: I do.

Leader: Do you believe in the Holy Spirit, the Lord, the giver of life,
who came upon the apostles at Pentecost?

All: I do.

Leader: Do you believe in the holy catholic Church, the communion
of saints, the forgiveness of sins, the resurrection of the body,
and life everlasting?

All: I do.

Leader: This is our faith. This is the faith of the Church. We are proud
to profess it in Christ Jesus our Lord.

All: Amen.

*Rite of Confirmation*

Leader: You are about to receive the Gift of the Holy Spirit in Confirmation. You are to be witnesses before all the world and your way of life should at all times reflect the goodness of Christ. And so I ask you now:

Leader: Will you persevere in resisting evil, and whenever you fall into sin, repent and return to the Lord?

All: I will, with the help of the Holy Spirit.

Leader: Will you proclaim by word and example the good news of God in Christ?

All: I will, with the help of the Holy Spirit.

Leader: Will you seek and serve Christ in all persons, loving your neighbor as yourself?

All: I will, with the help of the Holy Spirit.

Leader: Will you strive for justice and peace among all people, and respect the dignity of every human being?

All: I will, with the help of the Holy Spirit.

## Closing Prayer

All: Renew within us the power of our Baptism and fill us with zeal for your gospel. Strengthen us to acknowledge Christ, so that we who are born in his likeness may journey on the path of salvation begun in our Baptism. We ask this through Christ our Lord. Amen.

Small-group activity

Break

### Gathering Prayer

All: Come Holy Spirit . . . .

## Second Conference: John 14:26

*"The Advocate, the holy Spirit that the Father will send in my name—he will teach you everything and remind you of all that [I] told you."*

## Ritual and Witness to Christ

### Gathering Prayer

All: Come Holy Spirit . . . .

### Third Conference: John 16:12—13

*"I have much more to tell you, but you cannot bear it now. But when he comes, the Spirit of truth, he will guide you to all truth."*

### Ritual and Penance Service

Here are some problems that young people struggle with when it comes to making right choices:

- I give in easily to peer pressure even when I know what is being done is wrong.

- Sometimes I feel lonely, rejected, scared, hopeless. I know the right place to go for help, but I like to take the easy way out.

- I know violence is never the answer, but I get angry easily and I forget the rights of others.

- Actions always have consequences, but I sometimes think I can beat the odds.

- Abuse of alcohol, drugs and sex is a serious problem today. I think I can handle it.

When I examine my conscience, have any of these situations been occasions of sin for me?

Recalling my baptismal promises is a good way for me to examine my conscience.

Now you will have the opportunity to receive the sacrament of reconciliation—an excellent preparation for the celebration of Confirmation

### Celebration of the Sacrament of Reconciliation

Leader: Let us bring our retreat to a close by praying together:

All: God our Father, no secret is hidden from you, for every heart is open to you and every wish is known. Fill our hearts with the light of your Holy Spirit to free our thoughts from sin, that we may perfectly love you and fittingly praise you.

Grant this through our Lord Jesus Christ, your Son, who lives and reigns with you and the Holy Spirit, one God, for ever and ever.

*Votive Mass of the Holy Spirit*

# Called by Name

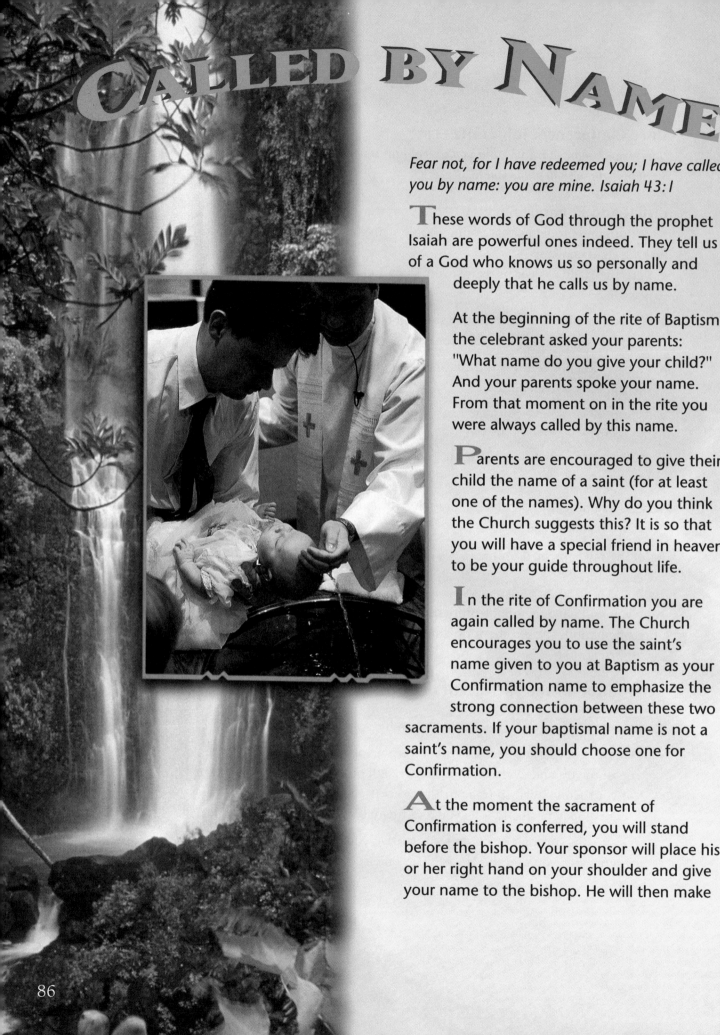

*Fear not, for I have redeemed you; I have called you by name: you are mine. Isaiah 43:1*

These words of God through the prophet Isaiah are powerful ones indeed. They tell us of a God who knows us so personally and deeply that he calls us by name.

At the beginning of the rite of Baptism the celebrant asked your parents: "What name do you give your child?" And your parents spoke your name. From that moment on in the rite you were always called by this name.

Parents are encouraged to give their child the name of a saint (for at least one of the names). Why do you think the Church suggests this? It is so that you will have a special friend in heaven to be your guide throughout life.

In the rite of Confirmation you are again called by name. The Church encourages you to use the saint's name given to you at Baptism as your Confirmation name to emphasize the strong connection between these two sacraments. If your baptismal name is not a saint's name, you should choose one for Confirmation.

At the moment the sacrament of Confirmation is conferred, you will stand before the bishop. Your sponsor will place his or her right hand on your shoulder and give your name to the bishop. He will then make

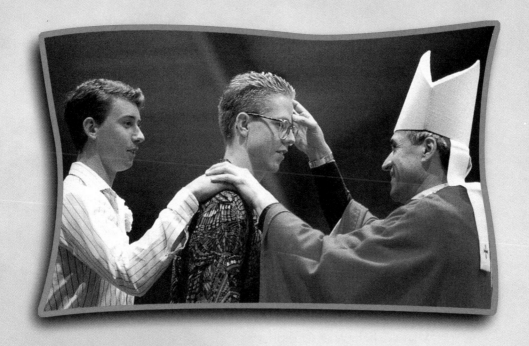

the sign of the cross on your forehead with chrism saying, "(Your name), be sealed with the Gift of the Holy Spirit."

## Making the Decision

Whether you use your baptismal name or choose a new one, it is important to learn as much as you can about your patron saint. After all, you are asking this saint to be your friend and advocate for the rest of your life.

There are many sources of information available on the saints. Your catechist will have some for you. Your parish school or library also may have books that will help you. An Internet search could be very interesting. Finally, speak with some adults whose opinion you especially value. Don't pick a name just because it sounds good or because it is popular. Take your time. Pray about it.

*Some names I am considering.*

*The name I have chosen is*

_____

*because*

_____

# I Believe

## Summary of Basic Catholic Beliefs

From the very beginning of the Church, Catholics have shared a common set of beliefs. One of the best-known statements of these beliefs is found in the Apostles' Creed. As you prepare for Confirmation, you may wish to use the answers to these questions drawn from the Creed as a review and reminder of what we believe as Catholics.

1. **What do Catholics believe about God?**

   We believe that God is the loving Creator of all that is and that each person is made in God's image and likeness.

2. **How has God revealed himself to us?**

   God is revealed to us as Father, Son, and Holy Spirit. We call this belief in three divine Persons in one God the mystery of the Blessed Trinity.

3. **Where do we find God's revelation?**

   We find it in Scripture and tradition, in the Church's living tradition of faith.

4. **How do we respond to God's ever-present love in our lives?**

   We respond to God's love through the gift of faith and by the way we live our lives.

5. **What do Catholics believe about Jesus Christ?**

   We believe that Jesus is the Son of God, the second Person of the Blessed Trinity, who became one of us to free us from sin and to bring us the fullness of God's revelation. Jesus Christ is the Messiah, God's anointed One, the Savior of the world.

6. **What is the mystery of the Incarnation?**

Incarnation means the unity of divinity and humanity in Jesus Christ. It comes from a word meaning "the putting on or taking on of flesh." Jesus Christ is fully divine and fully human.

7. **Who is the Blessed Virgin Mary?**

Mary is the Mother of our Lord and Savior, Jesus Christ. Some of the feasts on which we recall her part in God's plan are the Immaculate Conception (December 8), the Birth of Mary (September 8), the Annunciation (March 25), the Assumption (August 15), Our Lady of Guadalupe (December 12), and the feast of Mary, Mother of God (January 1).

8. **How did Jesus free us from sin?**

Jesus freed us from sin and brought us new life through his saving death and resurrection. In Jesus we receive grace, a sharing in God's life.

9. **What is the paschal mystery?**

We call the passion, death, resurrection, and ascension of Jesus the paschal mystery.

10. **What did Jesus promise on the night before he died?**

Jesus promised that he would send a Helper to be with his disciples. This is the Holy Spirit, the third Person of the Blessed Trinity. The Holy Spirit is also known as the *Paraclete*, or "Advocate."

11. **When did Jesus' disciples first experience the Gift of the Holy Spirit?**

The Holy Spirit came upon the disciples on the feast of Pentecost, fifty days after Easter.

12. **How are we initiated into the Catholic Church?**

We are initiated into the Catholic Church through the sacraments of initiation: Baptism, Confirmation, and Eucharist.

13. **What is a sacrament?**

A sacrament is a visible and effective sign given to us by Christ, through which we share God's grace. There are seven sacraments: Baptism, Confirmation, Eucharist, Reconciliation, Anointing of the Sick, Holy Orders, and Matrimony.

14. **What is sanctifying grace?**

Sanctifying grace is participation in the very life of God that brings us into an intimate and permanent relationship with the Blessed Trinity; we first receive this divine gift at Baptism.

15. **What is Baptism?**

Baptism is the sacrament in which we are freed from original sin, given a share in God's life, and welcomed as members of the Church.

16. **What is Confirmation?**

Confirmation is the sacrament that strengthens and continues Baptism; in this sacrament we are sealed with the Gift of the Holy Spirit.

17. **What is the sacramental sign of Confirmation?**

The sacramental sign of Confirmation is the anointing with oil with the words, "Be sealed with the Gift of the Holy Spirit."

18. **Who is the ordinary minister of Confirmation?**

The bishop is the ordinary minister of Confirmation.

19. **Who is the Holy Spirit?**

The Holy Spirit is God, the third Person of the Blessed Trinity, Lord and Giver of life.

20. **What are the seven gifts of the Holy Spirit?**

The gifts of the Holy Spirit are wisdom, understanding, right judgment, courage, knowledge, reverence, and wonder and awe.

21. **What is chrism?**

Chrism is a mixture of olive oil and balm blessed by the bishop.

22. **What is the Eucharist?**

The Eucharist is the Body and Blood of Christ, who is truly present—body, blood, soul, and divinity—under the appearances of bread and wine.

23. **What is the Catholic Church?**

The Catholic Church is the community of those who profess their belief in Jesus Christ as the Son of God, publicly affirm that belief through Baptism, celebrate it through the Eucharist, accept the teachings of Christ that have come down to us from the apostles, and carry out the sacramental life and mission of the Church under the leadership of the pope and those ordained in apostolic succession.

24. **What are we called to do as members of the Church?**

We are called to give witness to our faith in Jesus Christ through word and action. We are to be his presence in the world helping to fulfill his mission to bring all people to God.

# WE BELIEVE in one God,
the Father, the Almighty,
maker of heaven and earth,
of all that is seen and unseen.

We believe in one Lord, Jesus Christ,
    the only Son of God,
        eternally begotten of the Father,
        God from God, Light from Light,
        true God from true God,
        begotten, not made, one in Being with
            the Father.
        Through him all things were made.
        For us men and for our salvation
            he came down from heaven:
by the power of the Holy Spirit
        he was born of the Virgin Mary,
            and became man.
For our sake he was crucified under
        Pontius Pilate;
        he suffered, died, and was buried.
        On the third day he rose again
            in fulfillment of the Scriptures;
        he ascended into heaven
        and is seated at the right hand of the
            Father.
He will come again in glory to judge
        the living and the dead,
        and his kingdom will have no end.
We believe in the Holy Spirit, the Lord,
        the giver of life,
        who proceeds from the Father and the
            Son.
        With the Father and the Son he is
            worshiped and glorified.
        He has spoken through the Prophets.
        We believe in one holy catholic and
            apostolic Church.
        We acknowledge one baptism for the
            forgiveness of sins.
        We look for the resurrection of the dead,
            and the life of the world to come.
        Amen.

*NICENE CREED*

# COME, HOLY SPIRIT,
fill the hearts of your faithful
and kindle in them the fire of your love.

Send forth your spirit and
they shall be created,
and you will renew the face of the earth.

Let us pray.

Lord,
by the light of the Holy Spirit
you have taught the hearts of your faithful.
In the same Spirit
help us to relish what is right
and always rejoice in your consolation.

We ask this through Christ our Lord.
Amen.

*PRAYER TO THE HOLY SPIRIT*

# MY GOD,
I am sorry for my sins
with all my heart.
In choosing to do wrong
and failing to do good,
I have sinned against you
whom I should love above all things.
I firmly intend, with your help,
to do penance,
to sin no more,
and to avoid whatever leads me to sin.
Our Savior Jesus Christ
suffered and died for us.
In his name, my God, have mercy.

*ACT OF CONTRITION*

# HAIL, HOLY QUEEN,

Mother of Mercy,
hail, our life, our sweetness, and our hope.
To you we cry, the children of Eve;
to you we send up our sighs,
mourning and weeping in this land of exile.
Turn, then, most gracious advocate,
your eyes of mercy toward us;
lead us home at last
and show us the blessed fruit of your
womb, Jesus:
O clement, O loving, O sweet Virgin Mary.

*HAIL, HOLY QUEEN*

# LORD, make me an
instrument of your peace:
>     where there is hatred, let me sow love;
>     where there is injury, pardon;
>     where there is doubt, faith;
>     where there is despair, hope;
>     where there is darkness, light;
>     where there is sadness, joy.
O divine Master, grant that I may not
so much seek
>     to be consoled as to console,
>     to be understood as to understand,
>     to be loved as to love.
For it is in giving that we receive,
>     it is in pardoning that we are pardoned,
>     and it is in dying that we are born to eternal life.

*PRAYER OF SAINT FRANCIS*

# GOD, we pray for our young people,
growing up in an unsteady and
confusing world.
Show them that your ways give more life
than the ways of the world,
and that following you is better
than chasing after selfish goals.
Help them to take failure,
not as a measure of their worth,
but as a chance for a new start.
Give them strength to hold their faith in you,
and to keep alive their joy in your creation.
We ask this through Christ our Lord.
Amen.

*BLESSING FOR STRENGTH*

# JESUS, I feel within me
a great desire to please you
but, at the same time,
I feel totally incapable of doing this
without your special light and help,
which I can expect only from you.

Accomplish your will within me—
even in spite of me.

*PRAYER FOR LIGHT AND HELP*

# GLOSSARY

**Baptism:** the sacrament in which we are freed from original sin, given a share in God's life, and welcomed as members of the Church

**chrism:** a perfumed oil consecrated by the bishop during Holy Week and used in anointing those who are being baptized, confirmed, or consecrated in Holy Orders

**Christ:** the Anointed one, the Messiah; from the Greek word for "anointed one"

**Communion:** another name for the Eucharist, the Body and Blood of Christ; the sign and source of our reconciliation and union with God and one another

**Confirmation:** the sacrament that strengthens and continues Baptism; in this sacrament we are sealed with the Gift of the Holy Spirit

**covenant (biblical):** a solemn agreement between God and his people, legally binding on both sides and confirmed by offering a sacrifice to God or by a solemn ritual

**Eucharist:** the sacrament of the Body and Blood of Christ, who is truly present— body, blood, soul, and divinity—under the appearances of bread and wine

**gifts of the Spirit:** wisdom, understanding, right judgment, courage, knowledge, reverence, wonder and awe

**gospel:** an announcement of good news; in the New Testament the gospels of Matthew, Mark, Luke, and John announce the good news of salvation in Jesus Christ

**incarnation:** the union of divinity and humanity in Jesus Christ; word meaning "the taking on of flesh"

**Reconciliation:** the sacrament through which our relationship to God and the community is restored through forgiveness of our sins by Christ through the absolution of a priest

**sacrament:** a visible and effective sign, given to us by Christ, through which we share in God's grace

**sacraments of initiation:** Baptism, Confirmation, Eucharist—the sacraments that initiate us as members of the Church

**sanctifying grace:** a participation in the very life of God that brings us into an intimate and permanent relationship with the Blessed Trinity; we first receive this divine gift at Baptism

**symbol:** something that stands for or suggests something else

# PHOTO CREDITS

## Cover

Brian Fraunfelter: front cover (wave).

Crosiers/Gene Plaisted, OSC: back cover (chrism).

Panoramic Images/Naoya Nishida: front and back cover background (clouds).

## Inside

Franco Acornero: 58–59.

*Art Resource*/ 37; Erich Lessing:11.

Bridge Building Images, Burlington, VT 05402: 23 top.

*Catholic News Service*/ Michael Edrington: 64.

*Corbis*/ Arte & Immagini srl: 25.

*Crosiers*/ Gene Plaisted, OSC: 22 bottom, 23 bottom, 38, 39, 51, 52.

Christopher Talbot Frank: 68–69.

*FPG International*/ Richard Laird: 26 center; Telegraph Colour Library: 26 bottom; Benjamin Shearn 46–47; Ron Chapple: 53 bottom.

Brian Fraunfelter: 8–9, 12.

The Granger Collection: 50.

Anne Hamersky: 73.

*The Image Bank*/ White Lion Pictograph, Inc.: 30–31; Steven Hunt: 32–33.

*The Image Works*/ Will Yurman: 48.

*Index Stock Imagery*/ Shattil: 44–45; Fotopic: 56–57.

*Masterfile*/ Bill Frymire: 16–17, 28–29, 42–43, 54–55, 66–67, 78–79.

Abraham Menashe: 62–63.

*Natural Selection*/ Orion Press: 6–7.

*Photonica*/ Kamil Vojnar: 13; Mia Klein: 15; Pedro Leo: 34–35; Michael Allison: 36; Steve Marsel: 60 right; Wilhelm Scholz: 70–71.

*Sharpshooters*/ Joel Sartore: 10.

*Bill Slough*/ Our Lady of the Most Holy Rosary Catholic Community in Albuquerque, NM : 14 top.

*Tony Stone Images*/ Warren Bolster: 18–19; Andrew Hall: 20–21; Dale Durfee: 26 top; Olney Vascan: 31; David Young-Wolff: 40 bottom; Don Smetzer: 72 right; Pat O'Hara: 61 right; Mary Kate Denny: 77; Ian Shaw: 76 left.

*The Stock Market*/ Naoki Okamoto: 24.

*Superstock*/ The Grand Design, Leeds, England: 30 bottom.

*Sygma*/ Gianni Giansanti: 65; Bernard Bisson: 76 right.

Bill Wttman: 14 bottom, 27, 30 top, 40 top, 41.

*Zephyr*/ ICL: 48; Melanie Carr: 61 left.

# INDEX

Anoint(ing) 12, 20, 22, 29, 46, 50, 51, 54, 59
    with chrism, 47, 51
Apostles, 38, 51, 64

Baptismal promises, 30
Baptism, **6-17,** *13,* 41, 53, 59, 65
    and Christian community, 35
    effects of, 15, 23
    God's adopted children, 73
    grace of, 22
    infant Baptism, 22
    life giving waters of, 11
    new birth, 10, 11
    power of, 15
    symbols of, 11, 12, 13
    union with Jesus Christ, 15
    *See also* Sacraments of Initiation
Blessing, 35
    as ancient sign 37
Bishop(s), 27, 76
    as ministers of Confirmation, 38, 51
Blessed Trinity, 13, 23, 25, 27
Body of Christ, 41, 72

Candidate, 21, 35
Catholic, 16, 30, 61, 65, 73, 75, 77
Character, indelible, 23
Chrism, 22, *52,* 55
    anointing with, 50
    as sacramental sign, 51
    at Baptism, 12
    at Mass, 47
Christian community life, 27, 35, 46
Christian initiation, 73
Christians, 38, 39, 40, 52, 54, 63, 74
Church, 50
    activity of Holy Spirit in, 26
    and revelation. 25
    Body of Christ, 41
    community of, 37
    early, 64. 74
    initiation into, 12, 15, 22, 73
    issues, 7, 77
    teaching on incarnation, 63
    unity in the, 72, 73
Chrysostom, Saint John, 64
Community, 35, 37
Confirmation, **18-29,** *25,* 73, 74
    and Eucharist, 77
    bishop's prayer at, 65
challenges of, 76, 77, 78
    effects of, 23
    origin of, 22
    preparation for, 75
    *See also* Sacraments of Initiation
Courage, gift of, 20, 35, 39, 40, 59
Covenant, *73,* 74
Cross,
    daily, 36
    of Christ, 37, 41, 59
    personal, 40

Disciple, 20, 21, 26, 36, 37, 60, 61, 63, 64
Discipleship, 36, 51, 63

Easter Vigil, 22
    in early days of the Church, 22
    use of oil of catechumens, 50
Eucharist, 22, **68-79,** 73, 74, 75, 77
    liturgy of, 26
    See also Sacraments of Initiation

Faith, 33, 36

Gift of the Holy Spirit, 18, 22, 28, 38, 51, 53, 54, 55, 64
Gifts of the Holy Spirit, 37, 42, 65
    seven, 20, 21, 34, 35, 38, 39, 40, 59, 70, 71
God, 24, 58
Godparents, 30
Gospel, 41, 46, *63,* 64
    challenge of, 76
Grace, See Sanctifying Grace

Holy Communion, 73, 75
Holy Spirit,
    Advocate, 24
    as Gift, 22, 26, 38, 51, 53, 64
    gifts of, 26, 27, 38, 39
    Giver of life, 25
    guidance of, 37, 76
    help of, 41
    in Baptism, 13
    presence of, 37
    promise of Jesus, 24
    seal of the, 23
    Spirit of truth, 24
    Spirit of glory, 24
    strength of, 40
    third Person of Trinity, 23
    to understand the, 23

Immersion, 12, 15
Incarnation, *63*
Indelible character, 23
    *See also* spiritual mark
Initiation, Christian,
    *See* Sacraments of Initiation

Jesus Christ,
    acts of, 74
    Bread of life, 75
    command to love, 61
    community of, 37
    cross of, 41
    disciple of, 36, 37, 63
    friendship with, 60, 63
    incarnation, 63
    likeness of, 52
    mission of, 15, 26, 46, 53, 77
    promise of Spirit, 26
    saving suffering and death, 25
    teachings of, 77
    union with, 15
    values of, 40

Kingdom of God, 10, 58
Knowledge, gift of, 20, 35, 39, 40, 59

Laying on of hands, 21, 22, 35, 37-40, 42, 59
Liturgy of the Eucharist, 26, *73*

Mass, *75*
Messiah, 49
Minister of Confirmation, 38
Mission, 15, 46, 53, 77

New commandment, 64
New life of grace, 12

Oil,
    common uses, 48
    for anointing, 49, 50
    of the sick, 50
    of Catechumens, 50
    with Gift of the Spirit, 51
Opening Prayers. See Prayer, opening
Original sin, 23

Parish community, 77
Pentecost, 26, 37,51
Pope, 13, 15, 41, 53, 55, 65
Prayer, opening, 6-7, 18-19, 32-33, 44-45, 56-57, 68-69
Prayers, 90-93
Priest, 38

Retreat before Confirmation, 80-84
Reverence, gift of, 21, 35, 39, 59
Right judgment, gift of, 21, 35, 39, 40, 59
Rites, 19, 64
    of Confirmation, 23, 38

Sacrament, 11, *13,* 22, 23
Sacramental sign,
    anointing with chrism, 51
    holy oil, 50
    water of Baptism, 11
Sacraments of Initiation, 15, 22, *25,* 73
Sacrifice, 74
Salvation, 8, 10, 45, 47
Sanctifying grace, *13*
    as spiritual light, 13
Scripture, 24, 25
Seal with the Holy Spirit, 23, 51
    *See also* anointing with chrism
Signs, 37
    *See also* sacraments
Spiritual mark, 25
    See also indelible character
Sponsor, 30, 31
Symbol(s), 14, 15, 23, 24, 37
    breath, 21; candle, 14, clouds, 21, 24, dove, 21, fire, 20, 25, 28; light, 13, 21, 24, 28
Transformation by Holy Spirit, 27
Trinity, *See* Blessed Trinity

Water, 14
    symbol of Baptism, 12, 16, 20
White garment, 12,14
Wind, symbolism of, 21, 25, 26, 28
Wisdom, gift of, 20, 34, 35, 39, 40, 59
Witness(es), 20, 26, 29, 35, 37, 41, 46, 59
    of Christ, 36, 53, 64, 77
Wonder and awe, gift of, 21, 35, 39, 40, 59

Understanding, gift of, 21, 35, 39, 40, 59

*Italicized numbers* refer to definitions.      **Bold-faced** numbers refer to chapters.